TRANSFORMATION
UNLEASHED

Paperback ISBN: 9798391821144

Hardback ISBN: 9798391821151

INTRODUCTION

In 16th century Japan, a young samurai named Sasaki Kojiro embarked on a journey to hone his martial arts skills. He was a dedicated student of swordsmanship, known for his swift and lethal technique called "Tsubame Gaeshi" or "Swallow's Return." Kojiro's prowess in battle earned him the nickname "Demon of the Western Provinces."

Although Kojiro was an exceptional warrior, he sought balance in his life, following the samurai code of Bushido, which emphasized the importance of both martial and cultural pursuits. In addition to his rigorous training in combat, Kojiro enrolled in a traditional tea ceremony school, where he met his instructor, Sen no Rikyu.

Rikyu was a renowned tea master and a respected figure in Japanese society, known for his philosophy of "wabi-sabi," which emphasized the beauty of simplicity and imperfection. Kojiro, captivated by Rikyu's teachings, dedicated himself to mastering the tea ceremony.

Throughout his studies, Kojiro also discovered the art of poetry and flower arranging. He became enamored with the elegance of "tanka" and "haiku" poems, which allowed him to express his emotions and experiences in a subtle, yet profound, manner. Additionally, he found tranquility in "ikebana," the art of flower arrangement, which taught him the importance of harmony, balance, and the appreciation of nature.

Kojiro's dedication to both martial and cultural arts made him a well-rounded samurai, earning him admiration from his peers and rivals alike. As a result, he was able to forge lasting relationships, leading to alliances and strengthening the bonds between his fellow samurai.

The loudest voices often drown out the wisest, and it's been happening for far too long. Having written over three hundred bestsellers, I know my superpower, and this special anthology is an effort to use my powers for good.

In this book, you're going to meet thirteen amazing entrepreneurs who are changing lives in the coaching space.

There is often a mistake made in the west. We believe that loudness is a sign of excellence. You're about to discover that some of the quietest voices are making the biggest changes.

There is a need to balance all areas of your life. Sacrificing health limits your business rather than grows it. If you're sick, then you can't grow your business. If you're depressed, you'll work slower and dread getting out of bed.

We've taking a wholesome approach to entrepreneurship and see the physical, spiritual, emotional, and relational as connected.

1

LOVE THY NEIGHBOR

GREIG WELLS

As an entrepreneur and business owner, I have encountered my fair share of challenges and successes. The journey to success is seldom straightforward, but filled with twists, turns, and obstacles that test one's determination, passion, and faith. Over time, I have discovered a powerful, purpose-driven approach to business that I believe is truly the key to lasting success: Love Thy Neighbor Marketing. This approach has transformed not only my business, but also my life and relationships with others.

Initially, like many other entrepreneurs, I focused solely on my own goals and ambitions. I was determined to achieve success by any means necessary, often at the expense of my relationships with others. However, as I began to experience the highs and lows of entrepreneurship, I began to question my approach. Why did things sometimes feel so difficult? Why did I have to fight so hard for every small victory? It was during this period of self-reflection that I came across the concept of generosity first.

The idea is simple: treat your customers, employees, and

partners with the same love, respect, and care that you would give to your closest friends and family members. This means genuinely caring about their well-being, listening to their needs, and going above and beyond to help them succeed. By embracing this approach, I have found that not only does my business thrive, but I also experience deeper, more meaningful connections with those around me.

While I've encountered challenges along the way, I've learned that these obstacles are not roadblocks, but opportunities to grow and learn. As I've faced each new challenge, I've reminded myself that I'm on this journey for a higher purpose: to serve others and make a positive impact on their lives. With this mindset, I've found the strength to persevere and continue pushing forward.

One of the most profound lessons I've learned through my journey is the importance of staying true to my faith and values, even when things don't go as planned. I've faced moments of doubt and uncertainty, wondering if I was on the right path or if I should change course. However, I've found solace in prayer and the belief that God has a plan for each of us. By staying true to my faith and values, I've been able to weather the storms and emerge stronger on the other side.

Throughout my journey, I have been blessed with a supportive community of like-minded individuals who share my passion. These relationships have been invaluable to my growth and success, providing me with the encouragement, inspiration, and guidance I needed to keep going. By surrounding myself with positive influences, I've been able to maintain my focus on my purpose and remain resilient in the face of adversity.

One particularly powerful experience in my journey was a virtual dinner party I hosted for members of my community. During this event, we shared our stories, experiences, and insights, fostering deeper connections and understanding among the group. I was moved by the vulnerability and authenticity of the participants, as they opened their hearts and shared their personal journeys with one another.

In the supportive environment of the virtual dinner party, we discussed the challenges and successes we had experienced, as well as our hopes and dreams for the future. One participant's story particularly struck me; she shared how a simple prayer had helped her find direction and purpose in her life. This prayer, which she recited daily with her husband, asked God to bless her and enlarge her territory, guiding her on the path to success.

The power of this prayer resonated with me, reinforcing my belief in the importance of staying true to my faith and trusting in God's plan for my life. It also served as a reminder of the power of community and the importance of surrounding ourselves with individuals who share our values and support our growth. The connections formed during this virtual dinner party were not only beneficial to our individual journeys but also contributed to the collective success of our community.

As I've embraced the Love Thy Neighbor Marketing approach, I've discovered that the most effective way to promote growth and success in my business is to focus on helping others achieve their goals. This might mean going out of my way to make connections for someone, offering guidance or mentorship, or simply lending a listening ear when needed. By placing the needs of others at the forefront, I've been able to create lasting, meaningful relationships that have contributed significantly to my success.

One example of this approach in action is the story of a young entrepreneur named Tyson. When we first met, he was struggling to gain traction in his business and was unsure of how to move forward. I took the time to listen to his concerns, understand his goals, and offer my support and guidance. As we worked together, I connected him with valuable resources and individuals within my network, empowering him to grow and succeed in his endeavors.

In addition to helping others achieve their goals, this methodology also involves recognizing and celebrating the contributions of those who support our journey. When a member of my team goes above and beyond, I make it a point to express my gratitude and acknowledge their efforts. This not only fosters a positive work environment but also encourages continued growth and collaboration among team members.

One instance where I put this into practice was when a team member played a crucial role in connecting me with Tyson. Though her role in the process may have seemed small to her, I knew that her efforts had a significant impact on my ability to help Tyson and make a difference in his life. By acknowledging and celebrating her contribution, I hoped to inspire her to become even more involved in our mission and to continue making a positive impact on the lives of others.

Loving thy neighbor is more than just a business strategy; it's a purpose-driven approach to life that fosters personal growth, meaningful relationships, and lasting success. By treating others with love, respect, and care, we can create an environment where everyone thrives, both personally and professionally.

As we continue on our entrepreneurial journey, it's essential to remain true to our faith and values, trust in God's plan for our lives, and surround ourselves with a supportive community of like-minded individuals. Through these principles, we can overcome obstacles, celebrate our successes, and make a lasting, positive impact on the world around us.

So, as you move forward in your own journey, I encourage you to embrace your neighbors and discover the transformative power of love, faith, and community. May God bless you on your path, and I hope that our paths will cross again soon.

When I first began implementing the Love Thy Neighbor Marketing approach, I faced numerous challenges and setbacks. I knew I wanted to build a business that was focused on helping others and making a positive impact, but the path to achieving that wasn't always smooth. Despite these obstacles, I learned valuable lessons along the way that contributed to both my personal and professional growth.

One of the initial challenges I encountered was finding the right balance between serving my clients and staying true to my faith. I wanted to create a business that aligned with my Christian values, but at times, it was difficult to reconcile those beliefs with the profit-driven nature of the business world. There were moments when I questioned whether I could stay true to my principles while still being a successful entrepreneur.

As I navigated these challenges, I sought guidance from my faith and realized that I needed to focus on creating value for others rather than just making money. This shift in perspective helped me reframe my business goals and strategies, allowing me to develop an approach centered around helping others succeed.

Another challenge I faced was dealing with negativity and skepticism from others. When I shared my Love Thy Neighbor Marketing approach with colleagues and peers, some were supportive, while others questioned the effective-ness of such a value-driven strategy. There were times when I felt disheartened by the doubts and criticisms, but I remained committed to my vision and continued to refine my approach.

Through these experiences, I learned the importance of perseverance and resilience. In the face of doubt and criti-cism, I focused on the positive impact I was making on the lives of my clients and the wider community. This motiva-tion kept me going and allowed me to see the true value of my work.

One of the most significant areas of personal growth I experienced was learning to be vulnerable and authentic with others. I discovered that by sharing my story and the challenges I faced, I could inspire others to pursue their own dreams and overcome obstacles in their lives. This real-ization prompted me to become more open and genuine in my interactions with clients and colleagues, fostering deeper connections and trust.

This approach has had a profound impact on the lives of those I've worked with and mentored. For instance, I recall working with a struggling entrepreneur who was on the verge of giving up on his business. By sharing my own expe-riences and guiding him through the principles of this method, he was able to turn his business around and achieve success. He not only improved his financial situa-tion but also developed a more profound sense of purpose and fulfillment in his work.

Another example involves a client who was hesitant to invest in her own growth and development. Through my guidance and opening her heart, she gained the confidence to take risks and invest in herself, ultimately unlocking new levels of success and personal satisfaction. She went on to become a health coach and functional medicine coach, making a tangible difference in the lives of her clients.

These are just a few examples of the transformative power of love. By focusing on creating value for others and staying true to my faith, I've been able to build a successful business while making a positive impact on the lives of countless individuals.

As my approach continued to evolve, I found that the key to its success lay in building strong relationships with my clients and community members. I realized that my role was not only to offer valuable services and mentorship but also to create a supportive network where individuals could connect, collaborate, and grow together.

One of the ways I fostered these connections was by organizing events and workshops for entrepreneurs and business owners in my community. These gatherings provided a platform for individuals to share their stories, exchange ideas, and learn from one another. The bonds formed during these events often led to new partnerships and collaborations, which in turn, contributed to the overall success and growth of the community.

As my business continued to grow, I also expanded my team to include individuals who shared my vision and values. By surrounding myself with like-minded people, I was able to create an environment where the generosity approach could thrive. My team became an essential part of my mission, as they not only supported our clients but also acted as ambassadors for our values and principles.

However, there were also moments of self-doubt and uncertainty along the way. Running a business is never easy, and there were times when I questioned whether I was doing enough or making the right decisions. In these moments, I relied on my faith and the support of my team and community to stay grounded and focused on my mission.

One particular challenge I faced was scaling my business while maintaining the personal touch and connection that had been so integral to its success. As my client base grew, I knew I needed to find ways to continue providing the same level of care and attention that had defined my love-first approach.

To address this challenge, I developed systems and processes that allowed me to streamline my operations and provide consistent service to my clients, without sacrificing the personal touch that was so crucial to our success. I also invested in ongoing professional development for both myself and my team, ensuring that we were always equipped with the latest tools, strategies, and knowledge to best serve our clients.

This new approach to business has not only impacted my business and personal life, but it has also influenced the way I approach philanthropy and giving back to my community. I've always believed in the importance of helping those in need, and as my business grew, I was able to channel a portion of my success into charitable causes and initiatives.

One of the projects I'm most proud of is the creation of a scholarship program for aspiring entrepreneurs from underprivileged backgrounds. Through this initiative, I've been able to provide financial support and mentorship to individuals who might not otherwise have had the opportunity to pursue their dreams. By giving back in this way, I'm able to extend the reach of my generosity, empowering others to make a positive impact on their communities.

In reflecting on my journey thus far, I've come to realize that the true power of love lies in its ability to transform lives and communities. By prioritizing the needs and well-being of others, I've been able to build a successful business that not only supports my family and team but also contributes to the growth and prosperity of the community as a whole.

As I continue to refine my approach and expand my reach, I remain committed to my mission of helping others succeed and fostering a spirit of love, compassion, and community in the world of business. I believe that by staying true to these values and principles, I can help create a brighter future for entrepreneurs and communities around the world.

In conclusion, the journey of implementing this approach has been filled with challenges, but it has also been incredibly rewarding. The personal and professional growth I've experienced has allowed me to make a meaningful difference in the lives of those I've worked with and mentored. As I continue to refine and develop my approach, I remain committed to my mission of helping others succeed and fostering a spirit of love, compassion, and community in the world of business.

2

UNLEASH YOUR VOICE
JONATHAN GREEN

In the movie The Ghost Writer, one of the few movies about my profession I might add, Ewan McGregor discovers his clients big secret and it costs him his life. He's the second writer hired for the project. The first one also died mysteriously in the middle of the project.

This is why I try to avoid any job where the first ghostwriter died mysteriously. I tell every client at the start of the project not to tell me any secrets they don't want in their book.

Sure I have my silence as part of the contract, but that doesn't mean I want to end up slipping off a cliff.

People often as why I still ghostwrite when my own books have done so well and the honest truth is I'm addicted. It's my greatest skill and their's something magical about finding the greatness in a client and then showing that greatness to the world.

It's really hard to tell your own story and balance between being honest without coming across as too prideful. Most people struggle to write about themselves in a way that feels genuine and interesting. That's my magic.

I've published my entire process in multiple books and training videos, so it's not a secret magic. Here's how I transform a client into a compelling protagonist in the story of their life.

First, I ask insightful questions. For a long time I thought my main question was something genius that I invented, until I met someone in another industry who's been asking the same question for years.

You don't need to come up with the insightful questions, you can search online to find really good questions to ask people. I'll give you a few here that I use.

- If you never had to work again and nobody would judge you, what would you spend the rest of your life doing?
- What's your favorite thing about yourself?
- What's the worst thing that's ever happened to you that I'm allowed to include in the book?
- What do you want someone to feel after reading your story?
- What makes you special?
- Why should I listen to you?
- Who do you want to help and how can you transform their lives?

The secret isn't the questions. They are just the foundation. My real ability is how easily I become bored. Most great books aren't great because of what was written, they are great because of what was thrown away.

Every movie ends up with scenes on the cutting room floor. They spend millions of dollars filming scenes that only end up on a Director's Cut DVD. If people still by DVDs. Maybe now it's a Blu-ray.

My goal when interviewing a client is to get them rambling. I want to speak as few many words per hour as possible. If I can ask one question and they go on for an hour, I'm ecstatic. From all that material, I keep only the interesting and throw away the rest. And believe me there is a LOT of boring in there.

A client recently gave me around twenty hours of video to use on his book. I kept around eight minutes of it. I still watched it all. Transcribed it all. It was great video content, but not right for the book we were creating.

That's hard to do.

My job is to make you likable. That means I need to find your weakness, your motivation and give people a reason to root for you. That's not always easy.

When someone is rambling, I can focus on my real job. Finding the interesting. Stop. Wait. Go back. What was the story about falling out of a tree? What was the story about almost drowning.

I don't know if I'm a genius or just someone with a really short attention span who has no tolerance for anything even slightly boring.

I've written over three hundred business bestsellers and I've read less than ten business books in the past ten years. Business books are my work. Why would I read one for pleasure?

I read a lot of science fiction and action books and thrillers and mysteries. Those are books that ONLY have the interesting. That's the magic that I'm chasing.

People will read a boring business book if there is some good information, but nobody will read a boring fiction book. That's the standard I hold myself too. Will someone enjoy reading this book even if they learn nothing?

Clients don't want to hear that because they really value their information. And I get that. But let's be honest. If I ask the last ten non-fiction books you read, you'll be able to tell me less than five facts from each of them. And I'm being generous. Most people remember ONE sentence from the books they like. And that's fine.

My job is to understand reading behavior and how people interact with books in order to get my client to their idea result. To turn their story into something memorable. Most people I work with want to create a book for a specific reason.

They might want to create a legacy for a loved one, build their reputation, get better professional speaking jobs or grow their mailing list. Each of these books is written in a completely different way. The goal of the book determines what should be included.

Most people writing a book for the first time don't think this way. They have something inside of them that they want to release and they pour their blood, sweat and heart onto the page.

The problem is that nobody cares.

When was the last time you read a biography? The last biography I read was about Patton. It was amazing. But I can't think of another one I've read since graduating college.

How about this. When was the last time you read a biography of a non-famous person? A person you hadn't already hear of before.

That's right. We don't read biographies of non-celebrities anymore. So I have to thread the needle of information and interesting to craft a story that you want to read.

Putting this book together was hard. I personally hate anthologies. There's always one story that's way better than all the others. You discover one author that you really like and go from their short story to their longer books.

I don't want that for this book. I don't want any one chapter to stand out as better than the others. I want this to be a narrative that flows together and has a cohesive logic. There is a method to my madness.

Each of the other writers in this book has a really interesting story. That's the first step. The second is that they are likable. I know. I'm a professional. A big part of a ghostwriter's job is making unlikable people likable. But it's a lot easier of they come from a place of passion for their audience.

I have pretty solid non-disclosure agreements with my clients, so I can't get specific. But I can tell you that I don't like all of them. But for this book, I had more control of the process and was able to select people who do different things that all make sense.

It's important to be a full-spectrum entrepreneur these days. You have to grow your business, take care of your health, maintain your family and find time for spirituality. The idea that we have to sacrifice health to grow your business or that the only way to become a billionaire is through divorce...well, that's not the kind of book I wanted to create.

That's the reason I bought together people who help entrepreneur's with different parts of their journeys. I have written two books on depression and I think I'll write one about my PTSD as well. I'm not quite ready to share that story but my entire family was almost annihilated eighteen months ago. I mean we go to the hospital with between 12 and 76 hours to live. I was the 12.

Most people who teach entrepreneurs only show the shiny part of their lives. They are always on stage and afraid to talk about the real story. I can't do that anymore.

Here's something you should know. Being a work from home entrepreneur comes with crippling loneliness which leads to depression and sometimes health problems. Not enough people talk about it. So when it happens to you, you think you're the only one.

But you're not.

It happens to everyone. You go from talking to loads of people every day to going days without talking. Words start to feel strange in your mouth. Much of the world got a taste of this during lockdown. It's brutal.

Everyone has a story to find. Not everyone can afford to hire me to find it, but that doesn't mean it's not there. There's something special about you. A story that needs telling. And maybe only one person needs to hear it.

What if you spend ten years writing your book? You pour a decade of your heart and love into it. And then it only sells one copy. Are you a failure? You didn't let me finish. What if that story saves someones life? It gives them hope and they decide not to give up?

If you can change one life. If you can bring a little light into one person's universe, then I say it was worth it. That's why I still work with clients. That's why I don't keep my methods a secret.

What if you steal my entire method. You rip off my entire process and write a book that saves someone's life? I hope you do. Because you might get the goal, but I get the assist. And those are the things that matter the most.

This book is about bringing together some amazing voice and also showing you that a short story can be enough to get your voice out there. I want to see the amazing within you. I want to find the magic in your story. Because maybe, just maybe, your story could be the one thing that stops someone from jumping off that ledge.

And I want to help you.

IF YOU WANT to learn more about unleashing your story on the world, please visit me at CelebrityGhost.com

3

TRAPPED IN BED

NATASHA MARANO

A t a time when I was bedridden and struggling with my weight, I never thought I would be where I am today - a pioneer in the bariatric community, helping people find the root causes of their struggles and empowering them to lead healthy, fulfilling lives. The journey I took to reach this point was difficult and full of surprises, but it all started with one decision: I wasn't going to live like that anymore.

My journey began at forty-six years old, weighing three hundred and thirty pounds. I was desperate for change and terrified that my life was meant to have me stuck in bed and being bound to a wheelchair for the rest of my life. I knew that I was meant for more. It was at this point in my life that I decided to undergo bariatric surgery. Little did I know that this decision would lead me down a path of not only personal transformation but also the start of a successful business helping others navigate the challenges that come with post-bariatric life.

The surgery itself was a whirlwind. As with many bariatric patients, I experienced drastic weight loss in the first few months. I felt a newfound sense of confidence as I began to shed the pounds. However, what I didn't anticipate was the emotional rollercoaster that would follow.

Post-bariatric life is filled with challenges that many people don't understand. For instance, while losing weight was a significant accomplishment, I had to deal with the constant fear of regaining the weight I had worked so hard to lose. I also faced unexpected emotional hurdles, such as feeling a sense of loss when I realized I could no longer rely on binge eating as a coping mechanism. It felt like I had lost my best friend.

As I navigated these challenges, I began to recognize the gap in support and guidance for post-bariatric patients. This realization led me to create a business focused on helping others through this unique journey. My goal was to provide the emotional support, education, and guidance that I felt was missing during my own experience.

One of the most significant challenges faced by post-bariatric patients is learning how to eat healthily and maintain their weight loss. After surgery, patients often follow a strict diet that gradually transitions from liquids to soft foods, similar to a baby learning to eat solid food. However, once the initial post-surgery period is over, many patients find themselves at a loss. There's a lack of education and guidance on how to maintain a healthy lifestyle, leaving patients vulnerable to reverting to old habits.

My approach to helping clients starts with understanding that the emotional aspect of weight loss is just as important as the physical. Many post-bariatric patients struggle with feelings of fear, anxiety, and loss. I work to create an environment where clients feel safe and supported as they tackle these emotions and learn new coping mechanisms that don't involve food.

One crucial aspect of my approach is helping clients relearn how to eat. Many people fear they'll have to give up all their favorite foods, but that's not the case. Instead, I teach clients how to make healthier choices and find balance in their diets. This includes understanding portion control, making nutritious substitutions, and finding ways to enjoy food without overindulging.

When I first decided to become a pioneer in this field, many doctors thought I was crazy. Even my primary physician said I was going into a business that was going to fail. But I knew I had to do it, and despite the obstacles and pushback, I started my journey by focusing on helping individuals. I wanted to show them that it wasn't their fault they were struggling, and that there was more to learn in order to be successful.

As I continued to explore and understand what we needed as a community after having bariatric surgery, my focus shifted toward helping bariatric medical departments improve the long-term success of their clients. This new direction made me feel like I wasn't up against big companies, and I became determined to get to the bottom of the problem.

The turning point in my journey came when I realized that the medical community wasn't focused on the long-term quality of life for their patients. Once a patient had lost weight in the first year, they were considered a success, even if they didn't reach their goal weight or maintain it long-term. This realization made me even more determined to help people achieve lasting success after their surgeries.

And so, I began to look at the other side of the journey - the life that came after transformation. I discovered that there was so much more to life than just losing weight. I went from being bedridden to surfing in the Pacific Ocean, climbing the Rocky Mountains, hiking volcanoes, exploring jungles, and fire walking. My life completely changed, and people started treating me differently. Before, I was invisible; now, people hold doors for me and seek my attention. It was a remarkable change, but it also came with its own set of challenges.

One of the biggest challenges was knowing that I had to be careful with my relationship with food for the rest of my life. I had to acknowledge my true emotions and desires, and be honest with myself about what I wanted. For decades, I had been a people-pleaser and a perfectionist, trying to escape the invisibility that came with being over-weight. But now, I could be true to who I was, saying no when I needed to and standing up for myself.

This new life came with a price, though. Some people might be afraid of the hard work required to maintain their weight loss, or feel like they have to give up their favorite foods entirely. However, I believe that you can have your cake and eat it too. It's about learning how to have a healthy relationship with food, allowing yourself to indulge in your favorites occasionally while still maintaining your goal weight.

To help my clients achieve this balance, I often compare the process to the way a baby learns to eat. Just as babies start with a liquid diet and progress to soft foods, we do the same after bariatric surgery. But eventually, babies learn to eat a variety of foods in moderation from their caregivers - and that's where most of us are left on our own accord..

My mission is to teach people how to eat right, allowing them to enjoy their favorite foods without gaining back the weight they've lost. It's not about giving up everything you love; it's about understanding your relationship with food and learning to make better choices.

One of the biggest challenges I faced during this process was the fear of losing everything I had gained. Knowing the consequences of my actions and that I could gain the weight back was both motivating and terrifying. But I also believe that there's strength in having this knowledge and experience.

People who have never struggled with obesity may not fully understand the challenges we face. They may gain weight as they age, but they're unlikely to reach the levels of morbid obesity that many of us have experienced. They don't have the same emotional connection to food or the same number of fat cells that are waiting to be filled. This gives us a unique perspective and understanding of the journey.

Living with the fear of regaining weight is similar to living with an addiction. It's a constant battle, but it's also a powerful motivator to maintain a healthy lifestyle. It may not be an easy path, but the lessons we've learned from our struggles make us stronger and more equipped to deal with challenges.

As I continue to help others navigate their post-bariatric lives, I believe that authenticity is key. It's essential to be honest with yourself about your emotions, desires, and struggles. By acknowledging and confronting these issues head-on, we can begin to build healthier relationships with food and our bodies.

Exercise is an essential component of maintaining weight loss and overall health. I work with clients to find activities they enjoy and can commit to consistently. This often involves trying different types of exercise to see what works best for each individual.

Another critical element of my approach is addressing the mental health and emotional aspects of post-bariatric life. It's not uncommon for patients to experience depression, anxiety, or even grief after surgery. I help clients recognize and address these emotions, providing them with coping strategies and guiding them through the healing process.

To maintain long-term weight loss success, I offer several tips for my clients:

1. Develop a strong support system: Surround yourself with people who understand your journey and can provide encouragement, advice, and a listening ear.

2. Set realistic goals: Focus on achieving small, attainable milestones rather than trying to overhaul your entire life at once. Celebrate each accomplishment, no matter how small.

3. Keep a food and exercise journal: Tracking your food intake and exercise can help you stay accountable and identify patterns or habits that may be hindering your progress.

4. Prioritize self-care: Make time for activities that nourish your mind, body, and spirit. This can include meditation, journaling, spending time in nature, or engaging in hobbies you enjoy.

5. Learn to manage stress effectively: Find healthy coping mechanisms that don't involve food, such as deep breathing, progressive muscle relaxation, or seeking support from friends, family, or a therapist.

6. Stay educated: Continually educate yourself on nutrition, exercise, and mental health. Stay up-to-date on the latest research and best practices to ensure you're making informed decisions about your health.

7. Be patient and kind to yourself: Weight loss and maintenance are not linear journeys. There will be setbacks and challenges, but remember to treat yourself with compassion and understanding as you navigate this process.

8. Seek professional help when needed: If you're strug-

gling with your mental health or need guidance on nutrition and exercise, don't hesitate to reach out to professionals who can provide support and expert advice.

9. Develop a sustainable exercise routine: Incorporate regular physical activity into your daily routine to support long-term weight maintenance and overall health. Choose activities you enjoy and can realistically maintain over time.

10. Embrace mindfulness and practice gratitude: Learning to be present and appreciating the progress you've made can help you stay focused and motivated on your journey. Celebrate your accomplishments and use them as motivation to continue working toward your goals.

11. Create a healthy environment: Set yourself up for success by creating a living space that supports your goals. Keep your kitchen stocked with nutritious foods, remove temptations, and establish a designated area for exercise and relaxation.

12. Stay accountable: Share your goals with your support network, track your progress, and consider working with a coach or joining a support group to help you stay on track.

13. Remember your "why": Remind yourself of the reasons you decided to undergo bariatric surgery and commit to a healthier lifestyle. Use these motivations as fuel to persevere through challenges and maintain your focus on long-term success.

14. Be adaptable: Understand that your journey will require adjustments along the way. Be open to change and willing to reassess your goals and strategies as needed.

15. Celebrate non-scale victories: Recognize and celebrate the positive changes in your life beyond the number on the scale. These can include improved energy levels, better sleep, increased self-confidence, and stronger relationships.

Building a successful business helping post-bariatric patients has been incredibly rewarding. As someone who has walked this path and faced these challenges firsthand, I feel a deep sense of empathy and understanding for my clients. I am passionate about providing them with the tools, guidance, and support they need to not only maintain their weight loss but also thrive in their new lives.

Looking back on my own journey, I now realize that while bariatric surgery was a catalyst for change, it was just the beginning of a much larger transformation. The lessons I learned, the challenges I faced, and the successes I achieved have shaped me into the person I am today. I feel grateful for the opportunity to share my experiences and insights with others, and I'm dedicated to helping my clients live their healthiest, happiest lives.

As I continue to help others on their post-bariatric journeys, I'm reminded of the power of resilience, determination, and self-belief. Our experiences shape us, and the lessons we learn from them can be invaluable in guiding us toward a healthier and more fulfilling life.

I am deeply committed to helping my clients navigate the complexities of post-bariatric life and supporting them as they work to achieve and maintain their weight loss goals. I believe that by focusing on the mental, emotional, and physical aspects of this journey, we can empower individuals to take control of their lives and create lasting change.

My own journey has taught me that success is not only measured by the number on the scale but also by the growth and transformation that occurs throughout the process. It is my hope that by sharing my experiences and the education I've gained, I can inspire others to take charge of their health, embrace their new lives, and experience the joy and freedom that comes with living a healthier and more vibrant life.

The journey after bariatric surgery is one of transformation and self-discovery. It's about finding balance in our relationship with food, learning to stand up for ourselves, and living our lives to the fullest. Though the road may be challenging, the rewards are immeasurable, and with the right guidance and support, we can achieve lasting success and happiness.

So, embrace your journey, acknowledge your struggles, and remember that you're not alone. Together, we can continue to change the narrative around weight loss and bariatric surgery and create a well deserved brighter, healthier future for ourselves and others.

TO CONNECT with and learn more about Natasha, please visit bariatric-lifestyle.com

4

THE REFERRAL TREE

GARY SARCHET

I realized very early on that it was essential to build strong, powerful relationships with my existing customers and turn them into my referral base. This is the cheapest customer generation strategy in both time and money. Focusing on referrals kept my from fighting rates and the competition, because they already felt very comfortable with me.

I began my foundation with my friends and family. Making sure that each of them understood exactly what I do for a living. Many of us are afraid to tell our social circle about a new venture until we are successful. This shyness is what causes new venture to fail. How can your friends and family send you customers when they don't know what you do?

Fear of asking for the business is the first hurdle. At first your family members may think that you're trying to pull them into multiple-level marketing. I worked for years as a loan officer at a bank. My only goal was to get everyone I knew the absolute best rates possible. Trying to help them save money and give them a better life by reducing their monthly payments so that they can enjoy more of their time and have more resources.

Focusing on referrals was my epiphany.

It's not a fast solution. Most people in business are transaction based. They are looking to close the sale and then find the next customer after that one. Their employer gives them sales targets and they only focus on this month's numbers. They never plan for the future.

But the right person can transform those transactions into long-term relationships. One of my customers was a realtor stayed with me for twenty-five years. In that time, I made well over a million dollars worth of commissions. That number is impossible from a single transaction. It's only possible over time.

He referred everyone he knew to me. I handled all of his children's mortgages. I took care of his friends. And I took care of their friends.

One transaction turned into dozens simply through the power of long term thinking. I made north of a million dollars working with him and he made even more than that. Realtors earn higher commissions than mortgage brokers.

That's the type of relationship we're aiming to get to, where your clients become really good friends and will do anything for you. These relationships can be wins for both of you.

When I was sick, he went to my house, picked up my young son, took him to golf practice, then to soccer practice, and then brought him to visit me in the hospital. Every day I was recovering.

That's the relationship that we want with our customers, where you're not just a number; you're a very large, integral part of their relationship.

Even though I no longer handle loans, I am still in

thought with many of the clients he referred to me.

Asking for business is scary. It's the hurdle that trips up so many people who have to handle their own sales. We are afraid to come across as a telemarketer, sleazy use care salesman or the dreaded multi-level marketer who is offering you the chance to start your own business.

My goal is to create a situation where I feel comfortable asking for the business.

Unfortunately, way too many people are transactional and move on as soon as the check clears. They don't have any system to follow up with their clients to build a relationship. They often feel like they haven't done a very good job and don't deserve to ask. That's a mental hurdle we need to eliminate right now.

If you close the transaction on time without complication, you should feel really look good about asking for referrals afterwards.

It's easy to say don't be transactional, but that's just not good enough. When you meet a new person, don't size them up for their potential to be a client. We've all been judged a little too quickly by someone who lost the sale for assuming we couldn't afford what they have. Instead, get to know each person. Ask real and meaningful questions about everything other than business.

Ask about their kids. How old are they? What are their main activities? You will be amazed how a parent's eyes light up when you remember their kids name, age and sport they play. Why are they looking to buy a house right now? What made this house their favorite?

You don't have to memorize it. You can write the information down on a contact sheet or user a personal CRM app on your phone. It will remember everything for you.

A while back I was at a Mariner's baseball game in the

beer line and the people in front of me turned around. They recognized me because I'd sent their youngest son a birthday card years earlier. They bought my beer. One little birthday card turned me from a stranger into a friend years later.

I had never met them before. They'd just seen my face on the card.

This was the start of a beautiful relationship that led to seven transactions with them and at least twenty transactions through referrals from them.

Asking for the sale can be scary. Getting to know people? That's not scary at all. Ask questions that aren't necessarily relevant to the transaction. I think of every conversation as a seven-layer burrito. The only way to get to the best part is to ask seven deep questions. Then you really find out the answer.

This is a conversation not an interrogation, so I share as much about myself as I ask. Hey, maybe they'll send some birthday cards to my kids too! Real conversations have a natural flow. A question and answer session feels unnatural.

You are trying to build a lifelong relationship here. That relationships is a tree with branches. That customer is the tree and all their referrals are the branches, and then the referrals from the other people are branches.

It all starts with one tree. As you do transactions for other people from that tree, you'll always go back and recognize the original stump. Let them know how much business they've sent your way and how excited you are to give each of them an amazing experience.

They don't always know that one of the leads that they sent you has blossomed into another major referral source. And if you don't acknowledge them, they tree will wither and die. Appreciate all the amazing referrals and how you're going to deliver for their friends, that way they feel good and appreciated and the relationship strengthens.

If you're stuck in a transaction mindset because you have quotas to hit each month, it can help to imagine a field of trees. Each transaction makes you $100. If you grow that tree the branches will deliver ten deals. Now that transaction has jumped in value to $1,100. Each of those blossoms and grows into ten deals and referrals. Now we're over ten thousand dollars.

Referrals can 100x the value of each transaction. That should get you excited.

You can be nice and make a lot more money. That's a win for everyone involved.

This visualization helps people to get comfortable with asking for referrals. All you have t to say is, "Gary, I wanna thank you for your transaction. I'm glad you think it went really well. Again, if you know anybody else that needs treatment like the way I've treated you, please make sure you refer 'em to me and I'll give them exactly the same treatment that I gave you."

That's what they want to hear. That's the big door opener for referrals. Right after someone has done a transaction, whatever your business, they will run into a ton of people looking for het same thing. It's like when you buy a new car and suddenly everyone seems to be driving the same car as you. It's not true, but you're noticing the car because it's your focus.

Going deep with your interactions is going to change your entire business. People who try this method become the top producers in every office, no matter the industry. They aren't competing on rates and pricing. They aren't competing at all.

They build relationships.

They don't have to spend as much time getting to yes as somebody that's very transactional. This allows them to actually do more transactions than somebody who's very transactional. They don't have to spend tons of money on advertising and marketing.

You've got a team of referrals working for you 24/7, and that's the joy of building those relationships. If you've got the right mentality and the right team of of referrers, market slowdowns don't affect you.

In the twelve months before writing this chapter, loan rates have jumped up quite a bit. 40% of the workforce in the loan industry has lost their jobs because they were transactional. They didn't treat their job like a career and now it's over.

Their numbers dipped in a down market, so the company let them go.

Most of the time it's not their fault. Nobody ever taught them what I'm sharing with you right here. The company focused on short term quotas which created a team trained to be transactional.

Most people I meet aren't looking for a mortgage. The average American needs three mortgages in their entire lifetime. What are the odds that one of the other parent's on my son's soccer team need a mortgage the same day I meet them at practice.

If you forget the power of the tree, you might have a friendly chat and then forget their names. But the real value in people is their network. It's the part that isn't visible. Don't think about what they can do for you. Just plant seeds that can grow into trees.

If I'm the only person they know who does mortgages, every time someone they know mentions they are looking for a mortgage, my name is going to come up.

My goal is to wow each and every one of my clients. I look at each client I had as a referral source and I always wanted to do a good enough job that they want to share the experience with their friends.

Most people look at the dollars instead of the relationship and they miss the bigger opportunity. Instead of looking at relationship, they're looking at how am I gonna close this guy to get my commission? And not, how can I wow this guy and get referrals?

When you get a coaching client, you wanna wow them, so they refer you to other people in their office or other people that they network with.

When you start a new venture it can be scary telling your friends and family and former coworkers. What if it doesn't work out? How awkward will it be when your business doesn't succeed and they ask about it?

But here's the catch-22.

The reason many new ventures fail is that same secrecy. If you don't tell anyone what you do, they can't send you any customers.

Don't wait until the end of the transaction to ask for referrals. Plant the seed early in the relationship so that it feels natural and expected when you ask for referrals after the transaction.

When you meet a new client, ask probing questions and get to know them. Once there's a commitment from the person to move forward with you, let them know you're going to be asking for referrals after the transaction. This puts pressure on you to deliver the most spectacular experience possible and they are now expecting the ask. It removes the pressure from trying to find the perfect moment to ask them. Here's an example:

"Hey Gary, I'm gonna do such a good job for you. You're

gonna really enjoy the process. As you know, buying a big ticket item is not a fun process, but we're gonna make it as as least painful for you as possible. But part of my goal during this relationship, is that at the end of the day, you're gonna feel comfortable referring your friends to me."

You're not asking for the referral yet. You're placing the seed and now you've gotta fertilize it.

If you say it early, you'll say it later. This seed puts you in a position where asking for the referral isn't an issue. It's gonna be second nature.

At the end of the transaction, I say, "Thanks for doing business with me. Hopefully you like everything we did. My goal during the transaction was to make it as seamless and pleasant for you as possible. Do you know anybody else in your sphere of influence that may need my services?"

Because you've already planted the seed, a lot of people will already have names in their head that they're gonna give you.

Once you've reached out to that person and they move ahead with you, you go back to the original client and say, "Hey Gary, thanks for sending me over, Paul. We're doing a transaction, but that wouldn't been possible without you. So thank you again. And you know, again, if there's any other clients that you know that need my services, please forward my name to them."

You're always going back and thanking them which keeps it in their mind that they're looking for referrals for you.

To CONNECT with and learn more about Gary, please visit RealPerformanceCoaching.com

5

EMPOWERED GENERATION
MARK ENGSTAR

S ixteen years ago, I lost my brother to cancer. Since then I've dedicated my life to changing the world one life at a time.

Originally, my goal was to help as many cancer patients as possible through donations and support for new research. My mission and heart have grown with a desire to teach the younger generations how to have a better life.

As I grow older, I think about my legacy. I have a deep desire to help people who grew up without advantage to learn how to develop generational wealth. How to change not only their lives but the lives of their children.

Our educational system far too often teaches the hardest way to achieve our goals. We are taught that a goal is worth more if you struggle on the way there. That's not how the wealthy operate. They teach their children how to work smarter rather than harder. Why work for ten hours when you can accomplish the same task in two?

We focus on teaching children to grow like plants, but we only focus on the visible. We focus on what's above the surface. The parts we can see. But the most important part is the roots. Without a deep foundation, a plant cannot survive and a child cannot thrive.

My big goal is to help people in need, especially orphans, become self-sufficient and create their own income. I want to empower them so that they don't have to constantly rely on begging for money.

One of the things I'm most proud of is the work I've done to help orphans become more self-sufficient. I've had friends who grew up in orphanages and saw firsthand how they were completely dependent on the state. The idea is to shift the mindset of the orphanage to become self-sustaining and revenue-generating, rather than being dependent on others. This way, they can survive and even thrive during tough times.

When I first started my charity, one of the major challenges I encountered was dealing with multiple setbacks in the development of my website. I invested a significant amount of money into the project, but time and time again, I faced disappointment with bad website developers. Some even took my money without delivering the work they promised. Despite these setbacks, I never lost sight of my goal to help others and continued to persevere.

I created a WhatsApp group for the orphans and started sharing knowledge with them. I knew that knowledge was powerful, and that was the best way I could help them at the moment.

I can't wait until we're actually making money for these orphans. They've asked for my help in setting up donation pages and bank accounts so they can receive funds from abroad. I'm currently in the process of setting that up with my board members on the charity so we can route the money back to them.

My legacy and my main focus are my charity and my

social enterprise. However, I needed to start other base companies and bring in certified business coaches, managers, and mentors to help me work on these organizations. Instead of working in the organizations, I can now work on them and lead from behind. I'll still be bringing in new companies once I set things up, as I'm also creating a crowdfunding site to work with my marketplace.

I want to start working on programs to help people get off government benefits and start their own side hustles. It's not just about giving them jobs; it's about teaching them to think differently and become entrepreneurs. I'm currently developing these programs and seeking funding to build out our website and launch our ideas.

Through all these endeavors, I've learned a lot about perseverance and the importance of sharing knowledge. Even when I faced setbacks, I didn't let that stop me from pursuing my goals and helping others. By sharing the knowledge I've gained and the resources I have, I've been able to make a real difference in the lives of those in need.

I'm excited about the future and the potential for growth and positive change that my charity, social enterprise, and various businesses can bring. By creating a new breed of entrepreneurs and empowering people to become self-sufficient, I believe we can make a significant impact on the lives of those who need it most.

One of the key lessons I've learned on this journey is the importance of collaboration and networking. By bringing together like-minded individuals, coaches, and mentors, we can create a support system that allows everyone to grow and learn from one another. This collaborative approach has helped me build a strong foundation for my charity and businesses, and I'm excited to see how it will continue to evolve in the future.

Another important aspect of my approach is adaptability. In the world of business and entrepreneurship, change is inevitable. Being able to adapt and pivot when necessary has been crucial to my success. Whether it's finding new ways to generate income or exploring innovative solutions to challenges, maintaining a flexible mindset has allowed me to stay ahead of the curve and continue making progress.

As I reflect on my journey as an entrepreneur, I realize that the path has been filled with challenges, growth, and rewarding experiences. I've faced numerous obstacles along the way, but each of them has taught me valuable lessons and shaped me into the person I am today. I've had the privilege of meeting and learning from incredible mentors and coaches who have guided me, imparted their wisdom, and inspired me to give back and create a meaningful impact on the lives of others.

These individuals have taught me the importance of resilience, adaptability, and the power of knowledge. They've also inspired me to pass on what I've learned to others, leading me to establish my charity and social enterprise.

My approach to building a successful business is centered around the idea of empowerment. Instead of simply providing financial support or handouts, I aim to equip individuals and communities with the skills and knowledge they need to create sustainable income for themselves. By teaching people how to think differently and fostering entrepreneurial spirit, I believe I can create a lasting impact that extends far beyond temporary assistance.

One key strategy I've employed in my charity and social enterprise is the development of an easy-to-use system for generating income. By simply sharing referral ID numbers and directing people to my websites, individuals can earn consistent residual income from sales. I've also created multiple ways for people to make money using this system, giving them the flexibility to adapt it to their unique circumstances and needs.

Through my charity, I also focus on sharing financial knowledge and life skills with the people I aim to help. Knowledge is an incredibly powerful tool, and by equipping individuals with the information they need to make informed decisions and take control of their lives, I believe I can foster positive change on a larger scale.

Some of the orphans have already started doing great things, like growing their own food and getting into hydroponics. They've also built their own dehydration units to preserve and store their food. They're not only learning how to grow and harvest vegetables but also how to store and process them. In the meantime, I've connected them with other charities that are struggling, so they can share their knowledge and resources.

By sharing their knowledge with others, these orphanages are now able to support themselves and contribute to their communities in a meaningful way. They're no longer solely reliant on external assistance, giving them a greater sense of autonomy and self-sufficiency.

As for the future growth of my organizations, I'm currently working on developing programs that will enable me to collaborate with governments and other institutions to help more people. I'm actively seeking funding to build out these programs and expand our reach, with the ultimate goal of creating a new generation of entrepreneurs who are equipped to overcome challenges and contribute positively to society.

In the coming years, I also plan to launch a crowd-funding platform that will work in conjunction with my marketplace. This platform will provide an additional avenue for individuals and communities to generate income and access resources they need to succeed.

My legacy, my charity, and my social enterprise are at the core of everything I do. I'm committed to continuing my work, empowering individuals, and making a lasting difference in the lives of those I help. The challenges I've faced along the way have only strengthened my resolve, and I'm more dedicated than ever to creating a brighter future for those in need.

As my journey continues, I recognize the importance of collaboration and building a strong network of partners, mentors, and like-minded individuals. By working together and pooling our collective resources, skills, and knowledge, we can achieve far more than any of us could on our own.

One of the key principles I've employed in growing my organizations is the idea of fostering a sense of community and shared purpose. By connecting individuals from diverse backgrounds, cultures, and experiences, I believe we can create a supportive environment where everyone can learn, grow, and thrive.

For instance, I've created a WhatsApp group where members of various charities can come together to share their knowledge, experiences, and resources. This platform has enabled individuals to exchange ideas, learn from each other's successes and challenges, and ultimately, drive positive change within their communities.

Furthermore, I'm actively exploring partnerships with educational institutions, non-profit organizations, and private sector entities to broaden the scope of our programs and increase our impact. These partnerships will enable us to access additional resources, expertise, and networks, which will further strengthen our ability to help those in need.

In addition to expanding our reach and impact, I'm also committed to constantly refining and improving the way we operate. I'm continually seeking out new ideas, technologies, and methodologies that can help us work more effectively, efficiently, and sustainably. By staying agile and open to innovation, I believe we can stay at the cutting edge of social entrepreneurship and continue to drive positive change in the lives of those we serve.

Another area of focus for me is nurturing and developing the next generation of leaders within my organizations. I understand the importance of having a strong team of dedicated individuals who share my vision and are passionate about making a difference. To this end, I'm working closely with certified business coaches, managers, and mentors to help cultivate the skills, knowledge, and mindset needed for success in the world of social entrepreneurship.

My ultimate aspiration is to create a ripple effect of positive change that extends far beyond my own personal efforts. By empowering individuals with the skills, knowledge, and resources they need to take control of their lives, I believe we can create a global community of change-makers who are dedicated to making the world a better place.

As I continue to work on my charity, social enterprise, and various businesses, I'm constantly seeking new opportunities for growth and development. I'm always on the lookout for new ideas, partnerships, and ways to make a bigger impact on the communities I serve. By staying open to new possibilities and embracing change, I believe we can continue to create lasting, positive change for those who need it most.

In conclusion, my approach to building a successful business and making a difference in the world centers around empowering others, sharing knowledge, and fostering collaboration. Through perseverance, adaptability, and a commitment to growth, I've been able to create a network of businesses and charitable endeavors that are making a real impact on the lives of those in need.

I'm excited about the future and the potential for even greater change and success in the coming years. With the right mindset, resources, and support, I believe we can continue to empower others, create new opportunities, and make a lasting, positive impact on the world. As an entrepreneur and philanthropist, my mission is to create a legacy of empowerment, education, and opportunity for those who need it most, and I'm committed to pursuing that mission with passion, determination, and a steadfast belief in the power of collaboration and knowledge sharing.

To CONNECT with and learn more about Mark, please visit linktr.ee/mark.engstar

6

SKIN IN THE GAME

JUSTIN DOUGLAS

Newly married, working like crazy, going to school full time and both of my little boys were diagnosed with special needs.

My neighbor worked for the state and he came over to let me know that parents of two children with disabilities have a 95% divorce rate. My first thought was how cool it is to be in the top five percent. Because their is no way my marriage is going to fail.

My wife was nervous because we were already struggling to keep it together. I saw real concern on her face and knew that I had to take action.

I couldn't be normal. I knew I needed something bigger in my life. I dove into personal development and coaching with both feet. I read every book, watched every video and attended every event I could find. I was a black hole absorbing as much knowledge about life, relationships and transformation as possible.

For the first time in my life, I found a place where I belonged. These were my people. I received so much from this world that I feel like I can't help but share.

At the same time I was on my journey of discovery, even more stress was thrown into my life. I was thrust into a new leadership position in my family's construction business. My entire life I said I would never go into construction. But it happened.

I felt tremendous pressure to perform and deliver. I didn't want everyone thinking that I had a position I didn't deserve simple because of the circumstance of my birth. Working my way up the company, I felt trapped. I didn't have the authority to change anything. I always promised that if I was in charge, things would be different.

I think we all say things like that, don't we?

One of the most significant events that occurred in my life was during 2008, there was an industry-wide slow down in construction. We had too many employees and there was no incentive for them to do anything productive. They would come into the shop and watch the clock until it was time to go home. They would put in their hours, maybe spend some time cleaning, but really they weren't doing anything productive.

We basically had thirty paid janitors on staff. No one wanted to cut costs by letting all these unnecessary workers go, but no one was doing anything to try and fix the situation. After draining most of the companies savings out, the cuts started happening... and I was put in charge of the process.

I vowed I'd never let anything like that happen on my watch, but things didn't get much better and I wondered if I'd ever even get an opportunity to run the business.

We all cut back to working 3 days a week. I had a mortgage and a young family to take care of. I started looking for work in any place that was hiring. It was so discouraging to realize that in spite of all the time and energy that I'd put into a college education, there weren't any positions paying much over minimum wage. The only place actually excited to hire me told me I could start delivering pizzas that night.

It was a challenging time for me, and I felt lost and confused. However, looking back now, I realize that it was also a defining moment in my life. Despite what I thought were noble and selfless sacrifices that I'd made to build the family business and provide for my own family, I had actually become totally dependent on the validation of others and too afraid to let anyone see my flaws.

I dove into personal development and entrepreneurship. I knew I had to find a way off the ladder I'd been climbing because I knew it was leaning against the wrong wall. I started working crazy hours and looking for any opportunity to build a side hustle outside of my life as an employee.

I learned a lot of hard lessons and spent a lot of time and money, not just on business ideas and tools and schemes. I also sought out books and coaches and programs to try and fix myself. I was living off of 4 hours of sleep and sacrificing my health and my relationships trying to find some magical cure that would fix it all.

Over the next couple of years, the business was getting a little better. The economy was still flat, but I was working like crazy and we had a bunch of great people who just kept doing their jobs. The company culture was pretty bad. When trust is low, then everything costs more and takes longer. I learned that from one of the many business books I'd studied, but was having a really hard time trying to figure out how to change anything.

Then it was my turn. I suddenly found myself running the company and decided to go all in. I dropped all my other endeavors and worked like crazy to make changes. I'd already seen so many incentive programs and management techniques that didn't work so I thought I'd just try to swing the pendulum and do the opposite. We grew sales over that 1st year period by almost 20% even though the market hadn't improved at all.

The problem is that at the end of that year I found that I had more full time employees than we'd ever had before, more trucks and equipment - a lot of it in worse condition than ever, and lower profits than we'd had in the last 5 years. The truly maddening part was that I was working 70-80 hours a week to try and keep it all together.

I felt like I was losing everything. Then my wife told me she'd considered leaving and it just broke me. I was praying for a miracle because I knew I couldn't keep living like this. A friend of mine introduced me to a leadership group and I plunged once more into the world of personal development, but this time more focused on character development and leadership - foundational stuff instead of techniques or quick fixes.

I approached my company with a completely new strategy. I focused on upskilling my employees and implemented a profit sharing program. I wanted them invested in the company and to have the ability to earn even during lean times. Constructions is a fickle and seasonal business. There are stretches of months or even years where there simply isn't enough work to go around.

Most construction happens during a short window of time each year. Things really slow down for large parts of the year and companies try different approaches to the problem. There are big costs associated with keeping employees on the books who aren't doing anything. There are massive training and retention costs and if you let go of those employees during the slow months you have to try and replace them when the work picks back up again.

I figured out that if I put everyone on partial commission it would lower our overhead and give us some breathing room on expenses.

The only way I could get the staff and my family on board was to give myself the highest exposure. I put myself at the highest level of commission. It's fascinating how much trust you can get when you put yourself in danger. Firemen don't have to build any relationship with anyone. They show up to the problem and have instant credibility because they put themselves in so much danger. You see that uniform and you think they are going to save you. You give them your total trust.

I had to put myself into maximum danger to earn trust. The culture can change very quickly when the employer makes themselves as vulnerable as the employees. There are books and books about ways to build relationship with your employees. This is the fastest way to do it. As soon as you can show them on paper that you're the most exposed, they are on your side.

Once they saw that I was the most vulnerable, I gave them two choices. They could choose a conservative mix of higher salary and lower commission, or a riskier mix of lower salary with higher commission. The conservative option has a larger guaranteed income while the riskier option had a lot more potential income. I let each employee decide how much control they wanted over their fate.

I pulled up their income from the previous quarter and showed how much they would have earned with each package. They were able to make a decision from real data. When you give people concrete data it's much easier for them to choose. Each employee was able to make an informed decision.

I had a different set of options for each level of

employee. It's not fair to try to give the laborer who is on the bottom, that doesn't have a lot of control of his day, the same level of risk as someone who has the ability to bring in more clients. The worker who doesn't do anything customer facing. It's not fair to give him a huge amount of exposure for commission because he really does have a lot of control over our sales numbers.

They are able to earn raises and bonuses by improving their certifications and the quality of their performance. They can leverage their training and skillset to make more money. They can learn new skills. But they aren't in a position where commission makes sense because they don't affect the overall numbers.

The person who is a level higher has a little more control, so their bonuses were partially based off of their own performance, but also the performance of their entire division.

It's really easy to incentivize the wrong thing. People are very good at figuring out how to beat the system. If you incentivize speed, quality will start to drop so they can finish faster. If you incentivize quality, speed will drop because they want to finish each task perfectly.

A lot of my ideas had failed so I knew I had to modify the system multiple times until I found the right incentives to maximize the performance of my entire team. I would love to say I got it right on the first try but that's not what happened. People will game the system if you don't set it up right and it took my multiple tries to get it right.

I was transparent about the process. I made sure that everyone knew that I was committed to the outcome and that the process might need to be adjusted so that we could make it happen. Surprisingly they seemed more engaged and willing to communicate their perspectives and ideas.

They started doing all the things that we had "trained" (nagged, pleaded, and threatened) on for years.

My process provided more income for the team and they become more invested in the success of the company. We were all sharing the risks and rewards together. I was always finding new books for my team to read to continue their education and improvement. While I love providing my workers with an income it also felt amazing to have an impact on their lives.

It's possible to find leadership fulfilling.

I found that having an impact was the most important part of my day. That's when I discovered my passion for coaching. I had always enjoyed helping others, and I realized that coaching was a way for me to make a real difference in people's lives. I decided to start my own coaching business, and I have been doing it ever since.

I have two paintings of trees in my office that define my coaching philosophy. The first is the Mastery Tree. The idea is that we are meant to grow in multiple areas of our lives at the same time, like the branches of a tree. While the branches my grow at different speeds, working on one area of our life does not mean we need to sacrifice everything else.

The second painting is the Tree of Knowledge. It reminds me that sometimes we have to go into the darkness to face the scary stuff and find our weaknesses.

Coaching has allowed me to connect with people on a deeper level and to help them achieve their goals. It has been a rewarding experience to see my clients grow and succeed, and I feel privileged to be a part of their journey.

Most of my clients are self-employed. They are business owners but they are really working in their business. They are so busy they don't have time to extract themselves from the business. They are so busy struggling through the normal business cycle, they feel the business is running them.

The first step is to get off the ladder and transform themselves into true business owners and leaders. To shift their identity so they can own the business rather than need to operate the business. I help them to see what they can do with effective systems and processes. They transform their businesses into assets instead of something they have to constantly babysit.

Once they step off that ladder it's possible to help create a compelling ladder for their employees to climb. The goal is to remove all friction from the ladder so that employees can move up quickly. With a clear path you don't have to search for perfect employees and instead nurture the team you have.

You can quickly build trust with your team and start attracting the loyalty that is missing from so many companies. This trust goes beyond just your employees and out into your clients and customers as well.

My clients quickly experience some pretty radical changes. I went through the same transformation with my construction business. I went from working eighty-hour weeks to putting in just ten hours a week, and our profits doubled and continued to grow. I have discovered the formula for making more money while working less hours.

Together we setup a really simple scorecard to measure their business and then we find the biggest opportunities to expand their profit margin. Where does the real profit go and what are the real costs of running this business? Then we structure an incentive program with their staff that rewards the right behaviors.

Most of my clients double their profit while working less

hours within six months. Their employees start taking on more responsibility because they are rewarded for this behavior. They no longer need to call the boss to make every decision as they are financially rewarded for making decisions that benefit the entire company.

With my own company the team was making about double industry standard and we were happy to pay it because even after the increased payout, our profits had doubled, they were handling all the problems and I only had to put in ten hours a week. It was a win for everyone involved.

One thing I have learned through my experiences is the importance of self-care. I lost my first marriage in large part because I neglected my own needs and focused solely on helping others. However, I soon realized that I needed to take care of myself as well in order to be able to help others effectively.

I make sure to take time for myself every day, whether it's going for a walk, working on a song, or just taking a few minutes to meditate. This helps me to stay grounded and centered, and it allows me to be fully present for my clients.

After I'd left my family business and lost my first marriage, I started to feel like I was letting people down, and it was really affecting my confidence. So I decided to started to try and focus my coaching more on helping people to improve their relationships and personal lives.

I had a lot of experience working with people and helping them to see their potential, so I felt confident that I could make a real difference. I started out small, with just a handful of clients, but word of mouth started to spread and before long, I had a thriving coaching practice.

One of the things that I'm really passionate about is helping people to overcome their fears and self-doubt. I think that so often, we hold ourselves back because we don't believe in ourselves enough. But once we can get past those limiting beliefs, we can achieve amazing things.

Another thing that I love about coaching is that it's so rewarding to see people transform right in front of my eyes. It's incredibly fulfilling to watch someone go from feeling stuck and helpless to feeling empowered and in control of their life.

As my coaching practice grew, I started to realize that I had a real talent for business as well. I was able to attract new clients and build up my brand in a way that felt really authentic to me. And I found that I loved the creative process of marketing and branding just as much as I loved coaching itself.

So I started to take on more business clients as well, helping them to grow their own companies and reach new audiences. I found that I was able to draw on my own experiences as a business owner to help others navigate the ups and downs of entrepreneurship.

Now, my coaching practice and my business consulting work have really come together in a way that feels very natural to me. I help people to build their own businesses while also empowering them to live their best lives.

Of course, there are always challenges along the way. Balancing the needs of my clients with my own personal life can be tough, and there are days when I feel like I'm running on fumes. But I've found and married the girl of my dreams and overall, I feel incredibly grateful to be doing work that I love and that makes a real difference in people's lives.

Looking back on my journey, I realize that the most important thing I did was to believe in myself. Even when I was struggling with addiction and felt like I was letting people down, I never lost sight of my own potential. And that belief in myself is what allowed me to build a successful coaching practice and business.

To CONNECT with and learn more about Justin, please visit Roots.MasteryTree.com

7

MIRACLES COME IN THREES
KENNARAE THOMAS

As a passionate and dedicated wife, mother, nurse and entrepreneur, I have always sought to make a difference in people's lives. My journey has taken me through various aspects and stages of life, ultimately leading me to discover one of my true callings as a mentor and coach for women. In this chapter, I will share my insights and experiences, as well as my unique approach to building a successful business that combines the best of both worlds – faith and personal growth.

From my childhood, I've had faith in a higher power, who I simply acknowledge as God. Over a decade ago, I began tapping into my faith in God to build and create a life of which I had only dreamed. The concept involved not just taking action but creating a miraculous life by tapping into heavenly power, taking inspired action, and acknowledging the awe-inspiring results. That led me to my passion for helping other women to thrive and to live fulfilled, joyful lives they love!

From the very beginning, I recognized the importance of personal development, the power of the mind, and taking courageous action. I have found that tapping into heavenly power amplifies and strengthens success – often in joyful ways beyond what was originally planned. It leaves you with a sense of gratitude, wonder, and awe. I have studied the principles of manifestation, the law of attraction, quantum physics, and learning how to harness the power of thoughts to create and manifest the life you truly desire. Add to that faith, and you begin to tap into grace, or heavenly power, with results that are strengthened and greatly multiplied!

I call this "bringing miracles into your life." Of course, we cannot control miracles, but we can certainly influence and welcome them! I have found three key steps to bringing a miracle into your own life. In general overview, the first step is spiritual creation, the second is physical creation, and the third is acknowledging/celebrating the miracles that begin to flow into your life.

Many people have different words to describe spiritual creation, such as manifesting, the law of attraction, vision boards, or even quantum physics. Spiritual creation does not exclude these, but accepts and builds upon them while at the same time, acknowledging and tapping into heavenly power. I have found this brings miraculous results beyond what was originally hoped for or expected.

One of the most profound miracles I experienced early on while still learning to combine faith with inspired action occurred during a particularly challenging time in my life. Fresh out of nursing school, I began my first job as a nurse. As most new nurses do, I found myself working the night shift. For several years, I diligently carried out my duties, but after some time, my physical health began to suffer due to the long hours and nighttime shifts. In my twenties, I realized the negative toll this lifestyle was taking on my well-being and decided I could not work another night shift. I was feeling overwhelmed by the demands of my job as a nurse, and I longed for a change.

One day, while visiting with my sister in her living room, I conceived the idea of becoming a vacation nurse. I imagined having just one patient from a kind, wealthy family and accompanying them on vacations. Although my sister was skeptical about the feasibility of my dream job, I could not help but pursue it. I knew that I wanted to create a life where I could travel, work with kind people, and make a difference in the world. However, I was not quite sure exactly how to turn this dream into a reality. Despite my uncertainty, I began to create in my mind and in my heart exactly what the "perfect" nursing job would look like to me. Without realizing it, I was beginning the process of spiritual creation.

I was not quite sure what inspired action to take, so I just took any action. I began talking about my dream job with everyone I knew, from friends, to roommates, to members of my church and community. I expressed my passion for becoming a vacation nurse and caring for one patient while traveling with a nice family. Within just one week of discussing my aspirations, an unexpected opportunity arose. At a community event in the park, a college student overheard my conversation and mentioned a well-known local family in need of a nurse. This family, prominent in our community and church, nationally and internationally, was not only wealthy but also kind-hearted.

I was thrilled to discover they were seeking nurses for temporary around-the-clock care. After securing an interview, I joined several other candidates and was ultimately hired. Driven by my goal to become the best nurse possible for this family, I was cheerful, dedicated, and hardworking. Within two weeks, the family's patriarch approached me with a list of dates for their upcoming vacations, asking if I could be their travel nurse.

Stunned and overjoyed, I jumped up and down joyfully exclaiming, "This was my dream!! This was my DREAM!!!" To this day, I am not sure who was more shocked, me or him. Ha! I had spiritually created the opportunity I desired, began to take courageous action towards it, and now within 3 weeks, had the chance to provide care and compassion for a wonderful family while accompanying them on vacations. It was as if God/the universe had answered my call and provided me with the perfect opportunity to fulfill my dreams!

This experience showed me the power of spiritually creating, taking inspired action, and then being grateful for and acknowledging miracles as they begin to show up in life. It inspired me to help others achieve their dreams too. I knew that many women shared my passion for personal growth, and I felt a deep calling to create a platform where we could come together, learn from each other, tap into heavenly power, take courageous and joyful action, and manifest our dreams into miraculous reality.

That was when I decided to transition from nursing into full-time coaching and mentoring. I quit my corporate nursing job and dedicated myself to creating a business that would empower women entrepreneurs to manifest their dreams and create the lives they truly desired.

I developed a unique program that gives women specific steps, speed, and support in combining faith with inspired action to build and manifest their dreams in their businesses and personal lives. We work together on spiritually creating, taking inspired action, and celebrating the miracles that show up in our lives. Ours is a group of connection, thriving success, gratitude, celebration, and FUN!

One of my favorite success stories involves a client who came to me seeking help with emotional eating. While this was not my specific area of expertise, I decided to apply the same principles of manifestation and spiritual creation to help her overcome this challenge.

We began by envisioning her desired outcome – a life where she was fit, happy, and able to enjoy precious moments with her children without being held back by compulsive eating. This vision lit a fire within her, and by the end of our coaching call, she had already experienced a decrease in her cravings.

What happened next was nothing short of miraculous. Within two hours after our call, I remembered a coach who had come into my life just the previous day who specialized in compulsive eating. I reached out to her on my client's behalf. To our astonishment, the coach not only agreed to take my client into her group, but she also offered to mentor her 1:1 pro bono!

I was amazed at how quickly the perfect solution had manifested for my client, and it reaffirmed my belief in the power of spiritual creation and inspired action. This is just one example of the incredible results that can be achieved when we tap into heavenly power to manifest the life we desire.

In addition to these personal stories, I have witnessed many other instances where the power of spiritual creation and inspired action has had a profound impact on the lives of those I work with. Women who have followed these steps have been able to create new opportunities for business growth, attract supportive and like-minded individuals, and experience a greater sense of fulfillment and satisfaction in their personal lives.

As I continue to work with women and teach them the

steps of faith-filled manifestation, I am constantly inspired by the stories of transformation and growth that emerge from our collaboration. One of my clients, of course, is me and each new success - whether for others or myself - serves as a reminder of the incredible power we all possess to create the lives we desire and fuels my passion for helping us all unlock our full potential.

To further illustrate the transformative power of spiritual and physical creation and tapping into heavenly help, let me share an example of a nurse who had been dreaming of starting her own business but was unsure about how to make this dream a reality. Through our work together, she became clear on her vision and began taking courageous inspired action, such as certifying in the specialty she desired and seeking mentorship from successful entrepreneurs. As she continued to follow the steps of spiritual and physical creation, she started to see doors opening and opportunities presenting themselves that ultimately led to the successful launch of her business. Then, within 6 months of starting her business, she connected with a top national identity in her business specialty and 6 months later, became their lead trainer!

Another example is of a client in her mid-40s who decided she needed to take faith-filled action to get physically fit. She imagined having the energy to keep up with children and living a long, energetic life. She also believed in God/a higher power and prayed for help and success to fulfill her dream. She then took courageous inspired action by joining a fitness group by whom she had been greatly intimated. She showed up for the group at 5:00 am and soon found elite athletes rallying around her and her success. She continued working diligently with the group, six days a week for nearly two years and found miraculous results. Not only did she lose 42 pounds, she also won the one-mile run and 2000 meter rowing contest...taking 1st place for women in her age group...AND 1st place in all age groups for all women! She then beat the head coach in a running/hills contest! She had hoped to get physically fit, and by tapping into heavenly power, her diligent efforts were strengthened and amplified, creating miraculous results!

These stories demonstrate the immense power of combining faith with spiritual and physical creation and the impact this can have on our lives when we commit to the process and believe in our ability to create the reality we desire. The key is to stay focused on our goals, tap into heavenly strength and power, take inspired action - even when faced with challenges or setbacks - and learn to recognize and acknowledge the miracles that begin to show up in life.

As I continue on this journey, I am constantly inspired by the women I work with and the transformations they experience. My mission is to help women entrepreneurs step into their faith-filled power, embrace their dreams, and manifest the lives they truly desire. Together, we're creating a community where faith-filled personal growth and professional success go hand in hand, and we support one another in achieving our highest potential.

The key to success in this journey is understanding the power of our faith, beliefs and thoughts and how they shape our reality. I teach the women entrepreneurs I work with to harness this power by following a series of specific steps, which I'll outline below.

1. Spiritual creation: Begin by envisioning your desired outcome in vivid detail. Imagine what your life would look like if you had already achieved your dream. Feel the emotions associated with this vision and truly believe that it

is possible for you. If you believe in a higher power, pray for inspiration in achieving what you spiritually create.

2. Talk about it: Share your dream with others. The more you talk about it, the more real it becomes, and the more likely you are to attract the right opportunities and people to help you manifest it.

3. Take inspired action: Don't just sit back and wait for your dream to materialize. Instead, take proactive steps towards making it a reality. Inspired actions are the best, but if you aren't sure about an "inspired action" a good rule of thumb is realizing any action is better than none. This might involve networking, seeking out new opportunities, or furthering your education in your chosen field.

4. Acknowledge and celebrate miracles: Think of miracles as good friends. The more you recognize and appreciate them, the more they tend to come into your life. As you work towards your dream, be mindful of miracles (big and small) and synchronicities that appear in your life. If you believe in a higher power, make sure to thank and give praise to God for these miracles. These are signs that you are on a bright path, and celebrating and acknowledging them welcomes even more miracles into your life!

5. Stay open and receptive: Trust that God/the universe is working in your favor and that everything is unfolding as it should. Remain open to receiving guidance and support and be willing to adapt your plans as needed.

6. Surround yourself with like-minded individuals: Building a supportive community is essential to your success. Seek out others who share your passion for personal growth and faith-filled action and work together to uplift and inspire one another.

7. Be patient and persistent: Manifesting your dream life takes time, effort, and dedication. Stay committed to your

vision, and trust that with persistence and patience, you will achieve your goals.

In conclusion, my journey as a coach for women entrepreneurs has shown me the incredible power we all possess to create the lives we truly desire. By combining the principles of faith-filled manifestation with passion and dedication, we can create a world where personal growth and lifetime success go hand in hand.

As you embark on your own journey towards manifesting your dreams, remember to trust in your ability to tap into heavenly power, your innate power of spiritual creation, and the limitless possibilities that await you as you follow through with inspired action. Embrace your potential, follow your heart, and be gratitude for and celebrate the miracles that unfold along the way. Together, we can create a brighter future for ourselves and those we serve and make a lasting impact on the world around us.

To connect with and learn more about KennaRae, please visit ThrivingWomenToday.com

8

THE PAST IS NOT THE FUTURE
MARY CHRISTIAN

Beneath the towering trees of a Virginian forest, I took my first breaths in a humble tent, my cradle in the heart of a cult. Our community was composed of earnest believers, their love for Jesus ignited by the fervor of the 1970s Jesus movement. However, as is often the case in cults, the leadership soon began to twist the very freedoms God granted us, imposing their distorted visions upon our lives.

One such twisted rule was the prohibition of play for children. Now, if you've ever met a child, you know their very essence is play. Yet, within our community, I was forbidden to indulge in this natural instinct. At the behest of the cult leader, I spent many grueling hours each day, confined to a chair, forced to sit motionless by his side.

Years later, during a healing session, a memory emerged. I couldn't believe it was true, so I asked my mother for confirmation. She somberly nodded, recounting how I was punished at the tender age of 18 months for engaging in innocent play. I had been captivated by a water droplet on the verge of falling from a spigot, the entire world reflected within its tiny, quivering surface. More and more fascinated by each droplet, I tried to fixate on the microcosm before me, only to be scolded and reprimanded for such a simple act of curiosity.

During these early years I learned that play was not acceptable behavior. Comparing my upbringing to the exuberance of my own three-year-old daughter, I see the stark contrast in how children naturally engage with their surroundings. When I asked her how she spends her days, her response was a joyful chorus of "I play!" She plays at everything- dolls, crayons, bikes, and bathtime- every moment filled with exploration and wonder. This is how children learn and develop, pushing the boundaries of their world until they are gently guided by their parents' wisdom.

In their boundless curiosity, children are fearless. They dance with abandon and care little for the confines of lines when coloring. As I watch my daughter, I am reminded of the stifled environment of my own childhood, and I find gratitude in my heart. For it is that very repression that allows me to appreciate the beauty and importance of play in my own children's lives.

As my fifth birthday approached, my parents made the courageous decision to leave the cult that had constrained our lives for so long. Breaking free from isolation, we embarked on a journey to reconnect with our estranged relatives.

Our first stop was California, the land of sunshine and warm embraces from my mother's side of the family. I vividly recall my grandmother's front yard, dotted with landscape rocks that sparkled with quartz. For the first time, I could pick up one rock after another, openly expressing my excitement without fear of reprimand. This newfound freedom—open play—ignited a love for the outdoors and nature that had been suppressed within me.

The next leg of our journey took us to New York, where my father's family awaited. Among them were two cousins my age, their eager faces lighting up as we arrived at Nonni and Poppi's three-story Brooklyn home. I was instantly captivated by the steep staircases that seemed to hold a promise of adventure.

As if in sync with my thoughts, my cousins launched themselves down the stairs, sliding on their bottoms with joyful abandon. They would race back up, only to repeat the thrilling descent. I hesitated for a moment, but then joined them, laughter filling the air as we spent hours on this exhilarating ride.

With each rock and each slide down the stairs, I began the process of reclaiming the simple joys of childhood that had been denied to me, although some damage had been done on my young mind. As firstborn taking on many adult responsibilities early and this inner messaging against youthful play, I would not fully embrace the beauty and freedom of play until early adulthood. A spiritual mentor, my pastors wife, spoke out, and it was as good as permission granted, "you will get your childhood back!".

Fast forward to my life now, and my mission is to help others reconnect with themselves and find their purpose through creativity. I give permission for creative play. My approach to this is multi-genre, encompassing movement, sound, tactile arts, painting, collage, creative writing, and journaling. It's a multi-sensory creative approach aimed at helping people overcome hidden fear barriers and connect with their physical bodies and voices.

I believe that the creative part of our minds is the aspect of our being that can hear God, the spirit of God that speaks to us in nuanced, open-ended ways. God communicates through all of our senses, from visions and fragrances to colors and sounds. By nurturing the creative part of our minds, we become more open to hearing the messages and guidance of God.

One of the main issues with our modern society is that we gradually limit creativity as we grow older. Children are encouraged to explore their artistic and musical sides, but as we become adults, we're pushed to focus on more practical pursuits. This stifling of creativity can lead to feelings of sadness, depression, and a disconnection from our true selves.

I've witnessed firsthand how difficult it can be for adults to reconnect with their creative sides. When I've asked people to simply play with colors or mediums without trying to create something recognizable, many struggle to let go of their preconceived notions of what art should look like. They often end up creating something that resembles a familiar object or scene instead of letting their creativity flow freely.

Dance and body movement are also crucial elements in my approach to freeing people from their shackles. Many people are disconnected from their bodies, and it's often easier for them to engage in coloring projects or other artistic activities than to truly move and dance. When I see people coming alive in their own skin through dance and movement, I know that they're making progress in reconnecting with their earliest, most childlike selves- their inner be-bopping toddler!

Creative expression has been linked to positive mental health in numerous studies. Engaging in creative activities can help reduce stress, anxiety, and depression, while also promoting overall well-being. Art therapy, for example, is a form of therapy that utilizes creative mediums like painting, drawing, or sculpting to help people express and process their emotions. This form of therapy has been found to be effective in treating various mental health issues and improving emotional well-being.

Similarly, music therapy and dance therapy can also have positive effects on mental health. Both forms of therapy allow individuals to express themselves and work through emotions, which can lead to better emotional regulation and stress relief.

In addition to therapy, engaging in everyday creative activities, such as writing, painting, or playing a musical instrument, can have positive effects on mental health. These activities can help individuals process their emotions, develop a sense of mastery, and boost self-esteem.

Our society is filled with quick fixes and temporary solutions for happiness, but we're missing out on the deeper sense of purpose and fulfillment that comes from truly being in touch with our creative selves. We live in a world of instant gratification, where we can satisfy our cravings at the click of a button. But this focus on short-term satisfaction leaves us disconnected from our greater purpose and the feeling of being truly alive.

Many young people go to college without a clear idea of what they want to do, simply because it's the expected next step. I believe that if children were encouraged to maintain their creative freedom and self-discovery throughout their lives, they would have a much stronger sense of their passions and goals by the time they reach middle school.

In other countries, the approach to education and personal development is often different, with less emphasis on following a specific track or adhering to societal expectations. It's important for us to reevaluate our own systems and consider how we might better foster creativity and a sense of purpose in our youth.

In my work, I focus on various formats to help people reconnect with their creative selves and break free from societal shackles. While I know that some coaches focus on one-on-one sessions, I've found that retreat-style events and workshops are particularly effective. The concentrated time spent in these settings allows for continuous growth and momentum.

During these retreats and workshops, I guide participants through various activities that allow them to explore their creativity, find their voice and reconnect with their physical bodies. The results are often profound, awakening long suppressed dreams as they are awakening parts of themselves that have been dormant, including their ability to hear God for themselves. It is my belief and my experience that when Creator God made us, it was with the ability to create – even co-create with Him. If we have lost creative expression, then we have lost the most genuine God-likeness part of us.

Not only is the voice of God vital, but so are the voices of others who see us as our best selves, and can speak life into areas that have been dormant with doubt. Just as my pastor's wife confidently declared over my life a reclaiming of my childhood, often we need to hear the voice of others in such a way. Retreats naturally lend themselves to an out of the norm environment, rapid social camaraderie, and many voices echoing my own: Permission granted! Play! Create! Explore! Be! The raw emotions that enter the room when a handful of adults make space for their fascinated and frolicking inner five year old selves is nothing but sheer beauty! It's an energy that's unequivocal, and it's full of honesty and fragility.

As an honest confession, even in my adulthood, after I began to explore reclaiming my childhood, I struggled with being a people pleaser and a workaholic; I was not making enough creative play time. If only I had realized then that lack of this play time was killing time. Creative play time is self-love time, self-care time.

For as long as I can remember, I have been an artist, a dancer, and an innovator. I used to resent my parents for not enrolling me and more classes that developed these parts of me. Moreover, with a generational stigma against unproductivity, and parents who were disconnected from me and each other emotionally, I focused my time on working really hard at things that my parents and society deemed meaningful. This was my search for significance and acceptance. Then came a pattern of overwhelm, and a backlash of rebellion in my desire to be free to be. Just be.

"Freedom" is the anthem that the soul cries through one's whole life. Unfortunately, in an environment that is stifling, though it can be self-made, rebellion is quite often the byproduct of the soul's search for freedom. Rebellion has a hardness to it, because it is birthed out of pain. Reactionary "freedom" isn't actually freedom at all, but it is a different type of self bondage. Regardless of our life circumstance, we can position ourselves into a mindset of freedom and thwart the hardness of rebellion. Rebellion actually stifles creativity in many ways. My own rebellion held hostage the beauty within me, and prevented healthy, deep connections with others. Moreover, it blocked my God sensors from interacting with Him in a meaningful way.

Throughout my journey into the freedom to be, I learned valuable lessons (usually the hard way) that became the foundation for my unique approach to helping others. I discovered the importance of self-discovery, heart healing, embracing creative play, and finding a greater purpose that transcends momentary satisfaction. I realized that by helping others break free from the shackles of societal expectations and hidden fear barriers, I could empower them to live a life of authenticity and purpose.

As I began to share my insights and experiences with others, I witnessed incredible transformations in the lives of my retreat and workshop participants. The common thread is that individuals get more clear on what they truly desire to do, and they gain some tenacity to do it.

I have witnessed people start businesses, ministries, philanthropic endeavors, write books, speak publicly, and more. When freedom is in the room, and creative ingenuity is cultivated, the sky's the limit!

One woman, for instance, had been struggling with the expectations of her family to pursue a traditional career path. After attending one of my workshops, she found the courage to follow her passion for art and eventually opened her own gallery.

As my work has continued to evolve, I found that the more I shared my own experiences and vulnerability, the deeper the connections I formed with my clients and work-shop participants. They could see that I had faced similar struggles and had come out stronger on the other side, staying ever vigilant for my own continued growth. This understanding created a safe space for them to open up about their own challenges and fears, seeing where they had silenced God's voice, and even rejected the creative God expression through their lives. Our vulnerable safe space allowed us to work together to create lasting change.

One of the most rewarding aspects of my work is seeing the ripple effect it has on those around the individuals I help. When someone begins to live a more authentic life, it often inspires others to do the same. This is evident in the story of a mother who attended one of my retreats. As she learned to embrace her true self, she became a better parent, leading her children to grow up with a stronger sense of self-awareness and the confidence to follow their own dreams. Another woman left an abusive relationship and began one of the most liberating and inspiring journeys to freedom.

I have also witnessed the power of community in my workshops and retreats. When people come together to support one another in their journeys of self-discovery, the collective energy and encouragement can be transformative. I have seen participants form lasting friendships, creating networks of support that extend far beyond the confines of the workshop or retreat itself.

My own journey, from an early childhood filled with restrictions to freedom and a life dedicated to helping others find their purpose and creative expression, has been a constant process of self-discovery and growth. By sharing my story and insights through my retreats and workshops, I hope to inspire others to look inward and reconnect with their best selves as created, creative beings, and learn to hear the whisper of Creator. Ultimately, it's through this reconnection that we can unshackle ourselves from limiting beliefs, find meaning, joy, and a true sense of purpose in our lives.

To CONNECT with and learn more about Mary, please visit www.elevate-create.com

9

ENTREPRENEUR ROLLERCOASTER

DAN WALKOVITZ

M y life and that of my family were transformed when I left a corporate job and became an entrepreneur. During these 40+ years as a serial entrepreneur, I have been transformed many times. Now that I coach entrepreneurs, I watch their lives transformed be the work we do together.

My entrepreneurial journey began when I was employed at a company that owned, among other subsidiaries, an amusement park ride manufacturing company. That company invented and sold thrilling amusement attractions such as inverted roller coasters and log rides.

They created the first upside-down coaster and sold it to a California amusement park (not Disneyland) for approximately $580,000. Including the cost of the coaster, installation, and promotion, the park spent $2 million prior to opening the ride. The park generated an each subsequent year They attributed that growth to the ride we sold them.

The ride manufacturing company, however, made a

mere 8% profit on the sale -- $46,000. That didn't seem to me an appropriate sharing of profits.

I proposed to my boss that we stop selling the rides outright; instead, I believed that we should place these high revenue generating rides in parks on a concession basis whereby we would share in the incremental revenue generated by the parks. I was confident this would yield the company much more profit.

My boss rejected the idea, explaining that it was contrary to the nature of the holding company. Determined to explore this alternative model, I asked my boss if I could pursue the idea on my own. He agreed as long as I did it on my own time. My first entrepreneurial venture was born: I raised money to purchase one (and ultimately six) attractions that we installed in various parks on a concession basis.

Since that groundbreaking venture, I've founded or co-founded numerous companies, each one a testament to my unwavering entrepreneurial spirit. I've come to understand just how important a strong, well-defined company culture is for the success of a business.

This realization was one of the most transformational experiences I have had as an entrepreneur. I now coach entrepreneurs on how crucially import it is that entrepreneurs/founders:

- define their core values
- create a document that explains them clearly
- create behavioral and situational questions to use when interviewing all prospective employees
- propagate these values to establish a company culture
- manage consistently to the culture

These values must be the north star that guides every decision and interaction of the company.

The transformation leading to my absolute commitment to core values and company culture occurred when I left my last full-time position.

While still working for the holding company that owned the amusement ride manufacturer, I was recruited by another of its subsidiaries as Marketing Vice President. The company sold computer time-sharing services (think a very, very early version of the Cloud). My job was to develop revenue from markets other than the single large $1.25 million contract that provided the lions-share of their business.

One of our other customers had created a software product for structuring municipal bond issues. I agreed to license that software from him. With this product, we entered the investment banking sector where bond issues of this type were an important aspect of their business. The software was unrivaled in the market. Within a year and a half, we were generating $80,000 a month, or $1 million a year, in revenue from that sector.

To support this large and growing business, we opened an office in New York. Russ was the only person supporting this market. He worked tirelessly, frequently on weekends and throughout the night, to accommodate the demands of these demanding clients.

The manager of the New York office communicated to me Russ's request for a second phone line for Russ's apartment. Given time-sharing technology, there was no way he could access the computer and converse with our clients simultaneously.

The cost of the new phone was $5/month. Given $80,000 in monthly revenue generated by the clients Russ was single-handedly supporting, it was a no-brainer for me. I authorized this seemingly minor expense without hesitation.

The president of the time-sharing company didn't see it that way. He confronted me about the phone line. Despite my explanation of how Russ was working on his own time often all night long and on weekends so we could generate $80,000/month in revenue, the president remained unconvinced.

I questioned him politely on my authority. I was concerned that if I could not approve a $5/month expense, where did my authority start and end. He explained that I had authority to make decisions as I saw fit, but with full knowledge that he could override them at any time he wanted. It was obvious to me -- I could no longer stay with the company.

I spent the next eight months figuring out what I was going to do next. As I converged on a plan for a new consulting company, I wrote a five-page document outlining how people should engage within the company, with clients, and with other constituencies.

This document was a direct response to the way the president of my former company had acted with me and others. It provided the foundation of the company culture – a term that wasn't recognized broadly until years later.

Originally, I shared the document with prospective employees as part of the interview process. Now, I interview using behavioral and/or situational questions that relate to my core values and share the document itself only after they are hired. I've come to understand how essential a strong, well-defined set of core values and company culture are for the success of a business.

Every organization has a culture. If a founder does not

define it, it will be defined by the people in the company. It will devolve into a culture based on a random mix of emotions, power struggles, and other issues to the point where the company will be unrecognizable to the founder.

Four years ago, my life was transformed again. I was eagerly awaiting the commercial release of a long-awaited software product our company had created. We were living with our daughter, helping with her newborn baby.

Our daughter overheard me talking to a couple of fellow entrepreneurs with whom I was sharing my thoughts on various situations they were facing. This led her to suggest that I find a way to monetize what I had learned from my 40+ years as a serial entrepreneur because of the value she had heard from my discussion.

Her words inspired me to harness my knowledge and expertise in a way that could not only benefit others but also create a new and sustainable income stream. Little did I know that her astute advice would be the catalyst for a whole new chapter in my entrepreneurial journey, as a highly experienced coach for entrepreneurs.

My coaching is not a structured program, but, rather, specific to need. I focus, though, in two areas:

1. entrepreneurs in the early to mid-stage of their entrepreneurial journey who need to create core values and a process for hiring, propagating, and managing to these values.

2. solopreneurs and entrepreneurs who are introverts who need or want to sell effectively but are uncomfortable doing so.

I recognized as I began coaching that entrepreneurs are often introverts who are uncomfortable selling but who need or want to sell effectively. I supplemented my culture focus with an offering for these type of entrepreneurs.

I share with them a selling system that optimizes the unique characteristics that most introverts possess and that will enable them to become outstanding salespeople. Introverts should not attempt to sell as if they were extroverts. Instead, they must capitalize on the unique traits that we as introverts possess. That's what my introverted clients learn to do and do well.

The selling process I share includes three primary elements.

First, initiate the interaction with a rapport building conversation that has nothing to do with why you are there. This creates a personal relationship. Then, establish your credibility as the basis for encouraging trust. Zig Ziegler, an outstandingly successful salesperson once said, "If people like you, they'll listen to you. But if they trust you, they'll do business with you".

Second, use probing questions to get to the heart of their pain. Ideally, their pain point will match with one of your differentiators, and that will provide a basis for the next step.

Third, tell stories. Jennifer Aaker, a professor at Stanford Graduate School of Business, has studied stories for over twenty years. She has concluded that "stories are up to 22 times more effective than facts alone".

As pain points are identified, assuming you can help, tell a story about someone you worked with who suffered from the same problem. Explain how you helped that person overcome the same pain this customer is feeling, and how they are now as a result. Do NOT tell them, tell them a story – up to 22 times more effective.

Currently, I find myself in the midst of my eight-week SELL Bootcamp -- two-hour sessions each week with introverts who want to become outstanding salespeople and who are benefiting from what we share and the role-plays we do each week.

Just last week, I received a video from one of the participants. He recounted how he had encountered a sales opportunity while having a general conversation. Thanks to the techniques and strategies he had learned and practiced in SELL Bootcamp, he was able to apply, step-by-step, the new selling process, ultimately resulting in a $5,000 sale. His excitement was palpable.

He went on to express his gratitude for the Bootcamp, explaining that he had previously worked with other very well-known coaches and gurus. In his words, "I have never learned anything as profound and meaningful as what I learned in Sell Bootcamp".

This story is testament to the remarkable transformation that can occur when one embraces new knowledge and applies it in real-life situations. There's an incomparable sense of joy and pride when I witness the success of those I've worked with, especially when my guidance has played a crucial role in their achievements.

Another inspiring story involves a young man with whom I have been collaborating. He spent eighteen years as a STEM and standardized testing tutor. He aspired to start a tutoring company using the unique tutoring process he had been applying with great success. Last June, we began working together to bring his vision to life.

Through diligent research, well-crafted marketing materials, and relentless dedication, he made significant strides in his venture. This past week, he took a bold step forward by launching promotional ads across three different social media. We regularly share ideas on ways to improve every aspect of the business.

Witnessing his hard work culminate in success fills me

with satisfaction. The knowledge that my input has played an important role in helping is, without a doubt, one of the most rewarding feelings in the world.

Given my 40+ years as a serial entrepreneur, I am amused by the ever-increasing number of young coaches entering the market. How can a 35 or 40-year-old coach who can't have more than 20 years of experience understand the intricacies of entrepreneurship. Insights come from years of experience where each new experience, each discussion with other entrepreneurs, each book and article read combine to create exponential growth in wisdom. That type of growth isn't there for those with only a few years of experience.

I advise other coaches to always be honest and clear about what they are qualified to offer and avoid embellishing your accomplishments. In my view, admitting to past failures or setbacks can strengthen your credibility as it demonstrates that you've learned from those experiences. If you haven't had the experiences, you will be hard-pressed to offer meaningful lessons from them.

Today, the barriers to entry for coaching are incredibly low. This has led to an influx of coaches without the requisite experience in the area they coach and other who are charlatans, claiming to have had a myriad of phenomenal successes. This makes it imperative that those seeking guidance vet their prospective coach in many ways and from many sources.

So, what are the key lessons that entrepreneurs can learn from my experiences? First and foremost: prioritize the development of the core values you want to guide the future of the company. Build from these a strong culture, hire based on the values, and manage consistently to those values and the culture.

Second, as a young entrepreneur, you won't have all the ingredients to make the company successful. Hire strengths where you are weak.

If you are an entrepreneur who is introverted, do not jump to hire a salesperson. The costs of that will exceed what you expect – monetarily, wasted time, decisions from which you will have to recover, and more.

Instead, recognize that you are the company's best sales-person. To sell successfully use your secret weapons as an introvert – the unique traits that most all of us possess as introverts.

Finally, remember that the world of entrepreneurship is constantly evolving, and there's always more to learn. Whether you're a seasoned entrepreneur or a new coach trying to make a difference, stay open to new ideas, learn from your experiences, and continue to grow both person-ally and professionally.

I have been transformed many times while pursuing my entrepreneurial dream. In each case, my eyes were open to events, and I capitalized on them. I did not ignore them. Similarly, those with whom I have worked experience their own transformations. As you pursue your entrepreneurial dream, be alert to opportunities. Don't disregard them because they are not within your original vision. This way, you too will be transformed in ways you never expect with great benefit to you and your family.

To CONNECT with and learn more about Dan, please visit https://bit.ly/DW_EntrepreneurPRO

10

RIDE TOGETHER

AIMEE BRITTEN

The power of the pen is unbelievable!

Modern technologies enable authors to crush historic barriers to creative expression!

Early in my life, the demands of writing for school projects were always dreaded and considered punitive. Of course, everything was written in "long-hand" with a pen and paper. Making any mistake meant you had to re-write everything from scratch. Multiple rewrites were routine.

Later, I experienced an amazing transformation.

First, I discovered the mind-blowing freedom, artistic power and potential impacts of creative writing!

Over time, I also discovered fantastic tools for "speed" and "storing drafts." This started with a typewriter and then, a computer with keyboard.

I have always believed that I am on this earth to help others and do good in any way possible. There is no single method or avenue for my mission. I seize opportunities as they arise. My purpose manifests in various ways: promoting positivity; providing companionship; supporting someone in need; offering gloves to someone shoveling snow with bare hands or, guiding individuals in effectively expressing their creativity.

Many people love the idea of being a "writer" but are intimidated by what that may actually entail.

Using my own transformative experiences as a writer and artist, I encourage others to release their creativity to the universe. Many individuals possess intriguing anecdotes and passionately wish to share them with the world. I especially delight in witnessing their personal transformations.

As a guide for closet authors, I empower those who believe they have a story or a book within them. For many, writing and becoming an author can be very complicated and overwhelming. The art of writing a story, a poem, a song, a book, etc. can be daunting. I act as a teammate to help them effectively convey their message. Others give up after being hindered by traditional publishing processes. With encouragement, guidance and practical support, I help them to resuscitate their dreams.

One of the primary services I offer is in the realm of writing, wherein I assist clients realize their writing goals and life purposes. My strategies are to simplify the process and eliminate roadblocks. Many people are unaware of how to begin writing, believing they need countless hours to devote to their passion. I demonstrate that progress can be made through realistic tactics and actions. This means consistent, manageable commitments—such as dedicating just thirty minutes a day, one day each month to writing. Over a year, this can lead to significant accomplishments, unhampered by limiting mindsets.

To facilitate this journey, I introduce my students to strategies that clear away mental obstacles and simplify their approach to writing. For instance, I recently held a writers' group session during which I provided a series of prompts, to which we all contributed. Each participant was given 20 minutes to craft a short story. Some finished in as few as six minutes and others desired an additional ten. However, they were all captivated by the experience of composing a complete story in a limited timeframe. All the resulting stories were different and inspiring. This exercise served as a model for the creation of longer narratives, illustrating the power of focused, incremental progress.

Recently, I began working with an enthusiastic student who had struggled for 15 years to complete a book to her satisfaction. After two more years with an editor, she pitched her work to traditional publishers, only to face rejection for another two years. Disheartened, she sought my guidance.

I advised her to approach the writing process with a fresh perspective. Instead of dwelling on the 20-year journey and her practice of dedicating three hours each day to 'writing', I suggested that she celebrate her passion in a different fashion. I encouraged her to honor her efforts, break down her book into chapters, and treat each one as a standalone short story. Initially, she was hesitant.

I introduced her to a writing exercise using prompts. Much to her surprise, she completed a piece in just six minutes. This brief but fruitful session allowed her to realize that she didn't need to commit three hours daily, to make progress. Whether it's six minutes or an hour once a month, she now understands that she can choose a schedule that doesn't disrupt her life, while still producing meaningful work.

With a simplified process and a newfound roadmap, she is now filled with pride and excitement, ready to embrace her writing journey with renewed vigor.

Many aspiring writers view the craft as a mystery,

believing they must emulate the likes of Shakespeare to be considered worthy storytellers. When they enthusiastically share their work, they receive feedback on a personal and emotional level. They often encounter negative feedback or rejection from publishers, which they misinterpret as a negative evaluation of the quality of their writing abilities. Consequently, they fail to understand the business aspect of publishing and alternative opportunities available to them.

People tend to harbor misconceptions about the publishing industry, expecting immediate success and acceptance. However, even massively successful works like Harry Potter faced multiple rejections before finding a home. To break through these misconceptions and explore different paths for their stories, aspiring authors need to connect with like-minded individuals and mentors who can help them grow and improve.

Surrounding oneself with positive influences is crucial. A coach can uplift, encourage, and help to identify opportunities, focusing on strengths while addressing weaknesses. Negativity breeds negativity, and it is essential to distance oneself from such influences.

Aspiring writers should also remember that the journey to success is gradual. They cannot expect to begin at the top. Even the most renowned authors started small, producing numerous drafts and learning from their mistakes. Amidst the rough drafts lie the gems that make their work shine. The key is to keep creating, embrace the process, and find positivity in the pursuit of one's passion.

A woman spent 15 years writing a book, only to face numerous rejections when she tried to get it published. Undeterred, she used the feedback from editors and reviewers to improve her craft. Initially perceiving their critiques as negative, she eventually realized that they were helping her grow as a writer.

Through this process, she refined her query letters and the book itself, cutting its length from 70,000 to 40,000 words. She restructured the narrative, shifting events to create a more engaging story. This journey proved to be an invaluable learning experience, and she went on to share her newfound knowledge in workshops for aspiring authors.

Ultimately, she left her day job to become a writing consultant, coach, and lecturer. Though she never secured a traditional publishing deal for her first book, she self-published it, using her experience as part of her teaching materials. This transformative journey took 15 years, but in the end, she found her own version of overnight success and a fulfilling new career.

People should write from the heart, leveraging their strengths in the process. If they excel at outlining but struggle with details, they should collaborate with someone who can fill in the gaps. Publishing is a team effort, involving various elements such as title selection, cover design, and layout. No one becomes an expert overnight, and even then, expertise is ever evolving, with trends and genres shifting continuously.

The purpose of writing varies, from commercial to personal expression. Creative writing differs significantly from technical or instructional writing. Regardless of the reason, the key is to just start writing, whether by pen, tablet or computer. The only way to learn and grow is through action and feedback.

Also, aspiring writers should join groups, collaborate with others, and learn from those who have walked the path before them. Following others' experiences rather than just their advice can provide valuable insights. Theory can only take one so far. It's the application that truly tests and proves its worth.

So, just start writing. Embrace the process, seek feedback, and continue refining your craft. Like a recipe that transforms over time, your writing will evolve, and you'll discover your unique voice and stories to share with the world.

Hope and encouragement serve as the foundation for personal growth and achievement. Perfection is not necessary; it's more important to complete your story, even if it contains mistakes. Details can always be fine-tuned and various elements polished later.

An anecdote from the life of a friend in the high-tech field illustrates this point. After transitioning from the military to a university coding course, this friend found himself in a large amphitheater with only one other student. Unnoticed by the chatting pals, . The professor arrived and began his lecture. To highlight limitations in software development, the professor drew a comparison between peanuts and elephants, asserting that an elephant could eat a peanut, but it was impossible for a peanut to eat an elephant.

Challenging the professor's assertion with a broader perspective, the friend suggested that the peanut could, in fact, consume the elephant after it died. The professor was not pleased with the interruption. However, the other students in the crowded lecture hall found it amusing, erupting into gales of laughter.

The idea fermented and this interaction haunted my friend. Eventually, it inspired him to write about a peanut consuming an elephant. The concept evolved into a writing process that took about 20 years to complete, as a poem.

Although he never reconnected with the professor, his experience sparked a passion for writing. The poem went on to win several awards. He began to regularly compose poetry and short stories in addition to his daily work in high-tech.

This illustrates how even the most unexpected moments can have a transformative effect on our lives. It can lead us down paths we never thought we'd take. A single spark, a single pen can have enormous impact.

Everyone has a story to tell, perhaps even a dozen. Writing is a powerful way to share ideas, information and stories. It allows readers to enjoy vicarious experiences and events, and the visceral emotions portrayed. When one shares their creativity through writing, they offer a gift to the reader.

11

A SOUND BODY

SONYA JONES

My journey in helping others achieve their health and fitness goals began with my own passion for staying fit and healthy. It's been a lifelong pursuit, one that became even more crucial as I cared for my ailing mother, helped raise my younger sister and provide loving, long-term care for my older sister who has special needs. I knew that my ability to help others depended on my own well-being, and that drove me to keep learning and growing in the field of health and fitness.

Throughout my experiences, I've noticed that many entrepreneurs struggle with their weight. The main reason for this is that they're high achievers who don't handle stress well. As high achievers, in many ways, they're always looking to achieve more, but they haven't developed the coping mechanisms for managing the pressure that comes with their ambitions. As a result, they often turn to food as a way to deal with the stress, which leads to weight gain and other health issues, plus the added stress of trying to eliminate the bad eating choices' effects that can hamper them feeling well enough to build their business consistently.

So, it's not only crucial to get happy with GETTING healthy, but it's also amazing and lifechanging to find happiness in BEING healthy long term. And this is a skill that I teach people.

One particular story that stands out is when I helped a musician avoid hip surgery by losing weight. This individual was a high achiever with a regular nine-to-five job, as well as a creative side that led him to pursue a career in music. Like many entrepreneurs, he was always doing more than necessary, whether it was practicing his piano or working long hours. This sedentary lifestyle took a toll on his hips, but with my guidance, he was able to shed the extra pounds, avoid the surgery and reduce excess stress.

When I saw the positive impact my assistance had on his life and the lives of others, I felt a deep sense of joy and calm. Not only did I know that I could help more people, but the gratitude they expressed inspired me to continue on this path.

In working with clients, I've encountered two types of people. The first group comes in with a specific goal in mind and focuses solely on achieving that. Unfortunately, this often means they don't fully embrace the changes necessary for long-term success and end up returning for help for the same changes again and again down the line. The second group is more open to the transformative process, and they're often surprised by the additional benefits they experience as they work consistently on their health.

A common challenge many people face when trying to improve their health is the belief that they don't have enough time. They often attribute their reliance on fast food and lack of exercise to being overwhelmed or confused. However, the key to overcoming this obstacle lies in learning how to organize their time better and embracing a healthier lifestyle.

My approach involves helping clients not only achieve their weight loss goals but also maintain them by packaging their lives in a way that's sustainable. Many people tend to live day-to-day, treating each day like a brand new recipe, even though they've already mastered it and that becomes their bad habit. By helping them recognize the skills they already possess and instilling the belief that they can make lasting changes, I empower them to take control of their health long-term and that becomes their achievement.

The journey to better health and wellness isn't always easy, but the rewards are well worth the effort. As I continue to work with clients from various backgrounds, I've come to appreciate the resilience and determination they bring to the table. Every individual has their own unique challenges and goals, but the common thread is the desire to improve their quality of life and achieve lasting success.

When working with clients, I've found that it's crucial to provide a supportive and nurturing environment. This begins by establishing trust and building a strong connection with each person. By truly understanding their needs, I develop customized plans that cater to their specific circumstances and guide them towards their goals.

Another essential element in helping clients is educating them about the importance of maintaining a healthy lifestyle. This goes beyond just losing weight or improving fitness; it also encompasses mental and emotional well-being. As clients progress on their journey, they often find that their newfound health brings about positive changes in other areas of their lives. This holistic approach to wellness encourages them to stay committed and focused on their goals.

I've also discovered the value of celebrating the small victories along the way. Whether it's hitting a weight loss milestone or finding the confidence to try a new activity, these moments of success help to build momentum and motivate clients to keep pushing forward. Recognizing and acknowledging these achievements is a vital component of the health transformation process.

Over the years, I've had the privilege of witnessing many incredible success stories. Each one serves as a testament to the power of determination and hard work, as well as the impact that a supportive and knowledgeable coach can have on someone's life. These stories also serve as a source of inspiration for me, fueling my passion for helping others achieve their health and wellness goals.

Case Study 1: Overcoming Stress-Related Weight Gain

One of my clients, a successful entrepreneur, struggled with stress-related weight gain due to the demands of running her business. In our initial consultation, we identified her primary challenges, including a lack of time for self-care and a tendency to turn to unhealthy coping mechanisms such as emotional eating.

Together, we developed a personalized plan that focused on stress management techniques, healthy eating habits, and incorporating regular exercise into her busy schedule. As she began to implement these changes, she not only experienced weight loss but also noticed improvements in her energy levels, mental clarity, and overall well-being. Ultimately, her transformation had a profound impact on her business, as she was able to perform more effectively and make better decisions under pressure.

Case Study 2: Balancing Work and Health for a Busy Professional

A high-performing professional came to me seeking

help with managing her demanding career and her desire to improve her health. She found it challenging to prioritize self-care amid long work hours and the constant pressure to perform at her best.

Together, we identified her main obstacles, which included a lack of time, limited knowledge of healthy meal options, and insufficient exercise. Our customized plan focused on time management strategies, meal planning, and finding ways to integrate physical activity into her daily routine.

As she began to implement these changes, she not only started to see improvements in her physical health but also experienced increased mental resilience and better stress management. This, in turn, enhanced her productivity and overall job performance. Her successful transformation not only impacted her health but also had positive effects on her career and overall life satisfaction.

Case Study 3: Empowering a Client to Take Control of Their Health

Another client approached me after years of struggling with weight gain, low self-esteem, and a lack of motivation to make changes. He felt overwhelmed and unsure of where to start in his journey toward better health.

Our initial conversations focused on identifying the underlying causes of his struggles and setting realistic, achievable goals. We then crafted a comprehensive plan that encompassed dietary changes, a progressive exercise regimen, and strategies for building and maintaining motivation.

Throughout our time working together, I provided the support and encouragement he needed to take control of his health. As he began to see progress, his confidence grew, and he developed the skills necessary to maintain his new lifestyle long-term. His transformation not only led to a significant improvement in his physical health but also had a positive impact on his mental well-being and overall life satisfaction.

These case studies demonstrate the potential for profound and lasting change when clients are provided with personalized guidance, support, and accountability. By understanding and addressing the unique needs of each individual, I can help them overcome challenges and build the foundation for a healthy, balanced life.

My approach to health and wellness coaching is built upon the foundation of understanding each client's unique needs and circumstances. I believe that there is no one-size-fits-all solution when it comes to personal health, and the key to lasting success lies in creating customized plans that address the specific challenges and goals of each individual.

The first step in this process is getting to know my clients on a deeper level. Through in-depth consultations and conversations, I aim to uncover their motivations, aspirations, and any potential barriers they may face along the way. By truly understanding their personal stories, I can tailor my coaching style and develop a plan that is both achievable and sustainable.

Once I have a clear understanding of my client's needs, I begin to create a tailored plan that incorporates various aspects of health and wellness, such as nutrition, exercise, stress management, and mental well-being. I take a holistic approach to wellness, recognizing that all of these components are interconnected and play a vital role in overall health.

Throughout the journey, my role as a coach extends beyond simply providing guidance and support. I also serve as an accountability partner, helping clients to stay on track and overcome any obstacles they may encounter. By maintaining open lines of communication and offering regular check-ins, I can help my clients navigate the ups and downs of their transformation with confidence and resilience.

My approach to health and wellness coaching is centered around the belief that every client is unique, and their journey to better health should reflect their individual needs and goals. By developing personalized plans and offering unwavering support throughout the process, I am able to empower my clients to make lasting changes that positively impact all aspects of their lives. Through this work, I am honored to witness the incredible transformations that can occur when individuals are given the tools and support they need to take control of their health and well-being.

As I look to the future, my hope is to continue expanding my reach and empowering more people to take control of their health. By sharing my knowledge, experience, and passion, I believe that I can make a lasting impact on the lives of those who are ready to embrace change and unlock their true potential.

In this ever-evolving journey, I remain committed to learning and growing, both professionally and personally. By staying up-to-date with the latest research, trends, and techniques, I can continue to offer my clients the best possible support and guidance. As the world of health and fitness evolves, so too will my approach, ensuring that I can help as many people as possible lead healthier, happier lives.

Ultimately, my mission is to inspire others to take the first step towards better health and to provide them with the tools, knowledge, and support they need to succeed. By working together, we can overcome the obstacles that stand in our way and create a brighter, healthier future for ourselves and those around us.

The experience of helping others transform their lives has been incredibly rewarding, and I'm excited to continue sharing my knowledge and passion for health and fitness. As more and more people find success in their weight loss journeys, the impact of my work continues to grow, making a real difference in the lives of those I help.

In conclusion, my mission is to guide and support people, especially entrepreneurs, in their pursuit of better health and wellness. By understanding the unique challenges they face and offering tailored solutions, I can help them overcome the barriers that stand in their way. Through my experiences and the stories of those I've assisted, I hope to inspire others to take control of their health and live their best lives. I believe good health is for everyone and everyone deserves good health. I help a person live their best health so they can live their best life.

With regards to building your health even stronger so that you can build your business even better where are you most stuck right now?

To connect with and learn more about Sonya, please visit Facebook.com/SonyaJonesHealthCoach

12

RACE TO THE TOP

GODWIN MORDI

ost of my clients are Fortune 500 CEOs and successful entrepreneurs who do not really have time to work out. A lot of them dedicate their lives to making money and building wealth, often to the detriment of their health. Health becomes a priority when they receive pre-hypertensive or pre-diabetic diagnosis. Fitness suddenly takes center stage in their lives. They don't have a lot of time, but they need to fix the issue, rather than take blood pressure and diabetes medication for the rest of their lives.

In the relentless pursuit of success, I often remind my clients that our most valuable asset is our health. Yet, ironically, it's also the one we most frequently neglect. The ability to rise each day and strive for wealth hinges on maintaining good health, but many seem to forget this fundamental truth. In the whirlwind of ambition, monetary gains take precedence over everything else.

The mentality of "I'll tend to my family and health later" is not uncommon, but it's ultimately self-defeating. In the end, some entrepreneurs find themselves burnt out, drained of every last ounce of energy. They come home from work with nothing left to offer, which can lay the groundwork for marital strife and divorce.

The tragedy lies in the fact that these individuals pour their best selves into their careers, leaving only the remnants for their loved ones. And sometimes, those left-over pieces just aren't enough to sustain a healthy family life.

Born and raised in Nigeria, my humble beginnings were marked by poverty. We lacked electricity, clean water, and the luxuries of modern life, including toys. But amidst this scarcity, I discovered a passion for soccer. Unbeknownst to me, this daily pastime was cultivating a healthy and active lifestyle.

As I grew older, my parents harbored dreams of me becoming a medical doctor. However, I soon realized that my active disposition wasn't suited for the confines of a hospital. Instead, I chose to pursue a career as a sports physical therapist. This path allowed me to work with Olympic gold medalists and FIFA World Cup champions, providing me with invaluable experience and knowledge.

Recognizing the global shift from rehabilitation to injury prevention, I ventured to the United States in 2009 to complete my master's degree in fitness. I established my practice in a Los Angeles gym, and soon, word spread about my unique and effective approach. As a result, I began to receive referrals from top CEOs and entrepreneurs, who, having reached a point in their lives where fitness became a priority, sought my expertise.

These high-powered individuals have world-class fitness equipment at home but often neglect it, caught up in the pursuit of wealth. With health slipping down their list of priorities, they faced the prospect of relying on medication for the rest of their lives. Desperate for results, they turned to me for help.

My passion for fitness now drives me to assist these busy entrepreneurs in making the most of their limited time. I am dedicated to helping them achieve their health and fitness goals, empowering them to lead healthier, more fulfilling lives.

The glossy images in magazines and the stars of TikTok may captivate your attention, but they rarely reveal the truth behind their impressive physiques and strength. As insiders in the health and fitness industry, we know the secrets they keep, but the public remains largely in the dark. Despite following the workouts and supplements featured in these publications, most people will never achieve the same results, which is a disheartening reality.

When it comes to preventing health issues and maintaining well-being, I always remind people that fitness is not a destination, but a journey. The allure of rapid weight loss, like shedding 10 pounds in two weeks, may tempt some, but I challenge clients to consider their long-term goals. Are they aiming for a temporary transformation to look good at a wedding or special event, only to revert to their old habits afterward?

I encourage my clients to pursue a more sustainable approach, one that involves building a lifestyle that helps them achieve and maintain their goals. By transforming the habits that led to their success into a routine, they can effortlessly maintain their ideal weight and health. It's this approach, focused on consistency and commitment, that offers the most lasting and genuine results, rather than seeking a quick, temporary fix.

When someone approaches me for guidance, the first question I ask is about their fitness goals. Surprisingly, 90%

of people don't truly know what they want to achieve. They find themselves caught up in TikTok videos, YouTube tutorials, and the lives of Instagram models, seeking inspiration from external sources.

However, I encourage my clients to define their own fitness goals, dispelling the common misconception that a six-pack is the pinnacle of health. I often use NFL players as an example—while some may possess chiseled abs, others, like offensive linemen weighing in at over 300 pounds, might not. Despite their large stature, these athletes maintain a low body fat percentage and are considered fit. This essential distinction is frequently overlooked in mainstream conversations about fitness.

Rather than focusing on superficial appearances, I emphasize the importance of cultivating a sustainable, healthy lifestyle that allows individuals to live free from illness or disease. By enjoying their bodies and leading productive lives, they can thrive both mentally and physically.

For me, my fitness goals revolve around my love for soccer and volleyball. The joy and satisfaction I derive from these sports fuel my motivation to maintain my physique. Every workout I design is tailored to help me become a better player in these disciplines, and my focus remains on being the best version of myself.

Unfortunately, many people lose sight of their own goals as they attempt to conform to mainstream expectations. It's crucial to remember that personal growth and genuine progress require a clear understanding of one's individual objectives and aspirations.

Many people fail to recognize that fitness is a science, not just an aesthetic achievement. When clients come to me, I draw upon my knowledge of human anatomy, physiology, and posture to create tailored fitness programs that cater to each individual's needs.

It's crucial to understand that at rest, some muscles contract while others relax. Ignoring this balance and diving into workouts without proper knowledge can lead to injury. A comprehensive physical fitness examination is the first step in identifying each person's unique needs, such as which muscle groups require lengthening or shortening.

With a solid foundation established, I then address the eight components of fitness: agility, speed, cardiovascular and cardiorespiratory endurance, power, strength, flexibility, balance, and coordination. Each of these elements is inter-connected, and neglecting one can impact the others. The human body functions as a cohesive unit, and a well-rounded approach to exercise is essential.

In human anatomy, we find agonist and antagonist muscle groups. When one muscle group contracts, the other relaxes. To maintain proper posture and alignment, it's crucial to maintain a balance between these muscle groups. Continuously focusing on one muscle group at the expense of its antagonist can lead to imbalances and potential injuries.

Understanding the human body's anatomical landmarks allows me as a Fitness Disruptor to guide clients toward correct posture and alignment. This comprehensive approach to fitness ensures that individuals can achieve their goals safely and effectively, setting them on a path toward long-lasting health and wellness.

Working with me, clients experience a remarkable increase in productivity, primarily due to my approach to stress management. It's crucial to understand the difference between stress and distress. Stress is a natural part of life, while distress is the harmful effect of poorly managed stress.

How one handles stress determines whether it becomes a catalyst for productivity or a barrier to success.

I teach my clients to recognize stress for what it is and equip them with strategies to overcome it. For example, exercise is an incredibly effective stress reliever. I design programs tailored to each client's lifestyle and preferences, ensuring they can engage in exercise whether they're sitting, standing, or lying in bed. This approach eliminates the all-too-common excuse of not having enough time to work out.

Even with just two minutes to spare, I can create a workout that is both efficient and impactful, provided it is done with proper posture to prevent injury. By addressing stress and implementing tailored exercise routines, my clients can unlock their full potential and thrive in their personal and professional lives.

Imagine this: after discussing relationships, divorce, and other challenges, you find yourself with newfound energy after a long day at work. Now, you can spend quality time with your spouse and children, strengthening the bonds within your family.

Moreover, maintaining your energy levels throughout the day and knowing how to revive them when they dip allows you to be more productive in your professional life. As a result, you can enjoy increased success at work and a stronger connection with your family.

In every aspect of life, from your career to your personal relationships, you experience a win-win situation, paving the way for a more fulfilling and successful existence.

Another aspect we want to explore is the science of fitness, which is often overshadowed by the prevalence of yo-yo diets and misinformation.

I often remind people that humans are designed to enjoy food, which is why diets tend to fail. Countless diets have come and gone, each claiming to be the ultimate solution. A few years ago, during the lockdown, the keto diet took the spotlight. However, it wasn't intended for everyone.

Originally designed for individuals prone to epileptic seizures, the keto diet aimed to reduce the frequency of these attacks by shifting the body's energy source from glucose to ketones. Weight loss was merely a secondary effect, not the primary goal.

Yet, when people discovered that the keto diet could help reduce body fat, they eagerly jumped on the bandwagon, eager to consume high-fat, low-carb meals. But this approach isn't sustainable; excess fat still accumulates in the body, and eventually, it will catch up with you.

TO CONNECT with and learn more about Godwin, please visit GodwinMordiFitness.com

13

DANCE IN THE RAIN

SANDIFLY HO

The pivotal moment that led me to where I am today can be traced back to my father's words of wisdom. I vividly recall the stories he would share with me as a child, always emphasizing the importance of following my dreams. This advice stayed with me, shaping my path as I grew up.

I remember the day I was at the airport, about to leave my family behind to go abroad for further studies and to pursue my career. My father, then 75 years old, pulled me aside to impart one last piece of advice that would leave an indelible mark on my life.

With tears in his eyes, something I had never witnessed before, my father, Sandy, urged me to always do what I love. He had achieved financial freedom through his business, dedicating his entire life to serving others and often neglecting his own desires in the process. At that moment, he realized the value of staying true to oneself.

He taught me that the most important lesson in life is to follow our inner wisdom and remain true to ourselves. It isn't about living someone else's life or walking in their shoes. Seeing my father so vulnerable, with tears streaming down his face, I knew that this was a lesson I could never forget.

There was a book I once read that recounted interviews with numerous terminally ill patients on their deathbeds. It revealed that the most significant regret people had before they died was not following their true selves. This realization stayed with me throughout my life, shaping my decisions and guiding my actions.

At the time, I was the lead designer in UX and art design at a prestigious company in Australia. I loved my work, but deep inside, I felt a calling, an inner voice urging me to discover something more meaningful. I couldn't quite put my finger on it, but it was a persistent sensation that something was missing.

This feeling was further amplified by the advice my father had given me about living true to myself, instead of merely following the expectations of others. Growing up in Malaysia before migrating to Australia at 17, I had been raised in a culture where we conformed to societal norms and always agreed with the opinions of others.

For years, I had been living my life according to what others deemed suitable, ignoring my true self. I felt trapped, as if I was confined within a box. Despite my high-paying job and working for a high-profile company, I couldn't shake off a deep sense of dissatisfaction.

Each day, when I returned to my empty home, I would sink into a state of depression. It was as if there was a mission I needed to fulfill, but I couldn't quite grasp what it was. Driven by this inexplicable inner calling, I decided to embark on a journey of self-discovery and exploration, determined to find my true purpose in life.

The driving force behind my journey was the desire to

live a life of purpose, one that was true to my inner calling. I didn't want to reach the end of my days with a heart full of regret, wondering what I had accomplished in my life. Taking a page from my father's experience, I chose to take a leap of faith, pushing myself outside my comfort zone.

My mission became to inspire women, including business leaders, managers, entrepreneurs, and mothers, to embrace their unique selves and live authentically. I realized that the most important aspect of this journey was trusting oneself, even when faced with the unknown.

In my culture, we were often taught to predict outcomes before taking any action. But as I delved into personal development, reading hundreds of books on the subject, I learned the importance of forging ahead with trust and confidence.

Another significant factor that brought me to this point was my husband's career. He secured an exceptional job opportunity in the United States, which allowed us both to embark on this new chapter together. By embracing change and challenging ourselves, we hoped to unlock our full potential and live a life true to our inner callings.

Part of my motivation for embarking on this journey was the realization that I needed to do something different. When my husband secured a job in the United States, I was faced with the difficult decision of whether to give up my job and move with him. My self-doubt and insecurities grew as I contemplated leaving the security of my monthly paycheck behind.

Upon moving to the United States, I discovered that I was pregnant with my first child. This brought new challenges, as I found myself in a foreign country without the support of my friends and family, who were thousands of miles away. My first pregnancy was a difficult and isolating experience, as I felt trapped in an increasingly darker emotional state.

During this trying time, I immersed myself in personal development. I studied extensively, earning certifications in mindset and leadership programs, as well as emotional intelligence. I attended live events featuring top mindset trainers and even underwent one-on-one training with Olympians, including athletes with disabilities who had overcome incredible odds to achieve their goals.

These experiences, along with the guidance of mentors and the support of new friends, fundamentally changed my perspective. I came to understand that, as humans, there is truly nothing we cannot accomplish if we set our minds to it. This transformative realization fueled my determination to live a life aligned with my true passions and purpose.

One of the most profound lessons I learned during this period was the importance of controlling both our minds and our bodies. As I navigated this new chapter in my life, I found myself unable to work in the United States due to visa restrictions. This unexpected obstacle led me down a path of personal growth and self-discovery.

My experiences during this time inspired me to help others tap into their inner potential. I developed a unique program called the "Shy Dance Project," which focused on guiding people to overcome setbacks and make a powerful comeback in a short amount of time. As a visual learner myself, I understood the importance of incorporating different learning styles to create lasting change.

The Shy Dance Project aimed to help individuals declutter their minds, challenge their limiting beliefs, and dispel negative emotions through an innovative, dance-based approach. I envisioned this program as a mini retreat, specifically tailored to accommodate the needs of busy individuals, like work-from-home moms who may struggle to find the time for traditional retreats.

By combining personal growth, learning, and self-expression, I hoped to create an accessible and transformative experience for those seeking to embrace their true selves and live life to the fullest.

I realized that for many busy individuals, especially those with children, it can be incredibly difficult to find the time and opportunity to unplug and focus on personal growth. With this challenge in mind, I developed an innovative program that brings a monthly mini retreat directly to people's homes. This approach allows participants to fully immerse themselves in the experience and engage their five senses, body movements, and mental processes in a transformative way.

The program integrates aspects of manifestation, psychology, and creative thinking with dance to create an interactive learning experience that goes beyond simply reading. By applying these concepts through movement and immersive activities, participants can effectively enhance their confidence and rapidly transition from setbacks to comebacks.

This unique approach to personal development offers busy individuals the opportunity to invest in themselves, increase their confidence, and overcome challenges in a convenient and accessible way.

People who work with me are typically women, including mothers and businesswomen, who feel stuck and lost in their lives. They may have financial stability, but still struggle to find clarity and a sense of direction. My focus is on helping these individuals overcome limited thinking, mental clutter, and negative beliefs and emotions that are holding them back.

Often, clients may have unresolved childhood traumas that they are unaware of, which create blind spots in their lives. These traumas can prevent them from trying new things and pursuing their true desires due to fear and past experiences. My goal is to identify these blind spots and guide clients in breaking free from the constraints of their past, allowing them to finally experience the freedom and fulfillment they deserve.

Everything that occurs during childhood has the potential to affect a person's emotions and behavior later in life. For example, one client shared her experience of being ridiculed for her English language skills when she moved to a new country. This criticism caused her to feel insecure and doubtful about herself, despite her previous success as a manager in Korea.

This negative experience became embedded in her subconscious mind, ultimately holding her back from trying new things and pursuing her true desires. It's crucial to identify and address these deep-rooted beliefs in order to overcome the limitations they create, allowing individuals to move forward and embrace their full potential.

In an effort to help women overcome their limiting beliefs and negative emotions, I have developed a unique program called Shy Dance, which combines personal growth and physical fitness in a virtual mini-retreat format. This program is designed to be easily accessible from the comfort of your own home, making it a convenient solution for busy women.

Shy Dance incorporates body movement and dance as a way to not only declutter your mind and address negative emotions and limiting beliefs but also to improve your physical fitness. This holistic approach helps participants save time while still focusing on essential aspects of well-being, such as exercise, proper diet, and increased productivity.

Through one-on-one sessions, the program aims to break through subconscious barriers and elevate participants' innovative thinking to new heights. Shy Dance offers an immersive, transformative experience that empowers women to overcome obstacles and reach their full potential.

After years of delving into the secrets of success, learning from numerous mentors, and experiencing both failures and triumphs, I've come to an important realization: it's essential to align our path with our future self and soul. As you contemplate who you are today, have you ever pondered how to unlock your true potential? If so, now is the time to step beyond your comfort zone and wholeheartedly embrace personal growth. Together, let's embark on a journey of self-discovery and explore the steps you can take to become the best version of yourself.

1. Shift your focus from advising your younger self to forgiving yourself for past decisions.

2. Recognize the limiting beliefs and inner critic that frequently emerge in the narratives we construct about our identity.

3. Trust in your current self and appreciate the accomplishments you have achieved thus far.

4. Envision your future self, aligned with your soul, and live as if you have already become that person.

5. Remember to enjoy the journey, no matter the circumstances.

. . .

TO CONNECT with and learn more about Sandifly, please visit https://www.sandifly.com/sandifly-8

14

TAKE AIM

MIKE HARRISON

You might know people who miss a lot in their lives - at home, at work, or in their hobbies. It can feel like they're not really living, just existing. This coaching seminar aims to make a great difference in your life and the lives of others, and I'm really excited about it.

I enjoy coaching busy executives who want to balance work and family life, as well as entrepreneurs with numerous great ideas. Helping people gain clarity on their goals and aspirations is a passion of mine, and I'm not afraid to be honest with them.

Our lives are divided into many segments - work, family, hobbies, relationships, and sports. For many, life seems fragmented, disordered, and divided. What if we could bring all these facets together in perfect balance and harmony? That would be an absolute miracle. To achieve this, it's crucial to focus on three essential components: making an impact, creating income flow, and developing intimacy with a few while influencing many.

Since you're reading this, living a spectacular life is important to you. You probably know what to do to achieve that, and you're very capable. But what makes it difficult to accomplish your goals? What prevents you from doing what you know you should? There's a significant distance between knowing and doing, and understanding the change process is key.

The change process can be broken down into three levels:

1. Knowledge: "What I know."
2. Attitude: "What I feel."
3. Behavior: "What I do."

You see, between knowledge and behavior—what I know and what I do—is attitude, "what I feel." Attitude is a crucial aspect of success. A positive attitude makes all the difference in the world, as it can determine how far you can go in life. Surrounding yourself with positive influences is invaluable, as it can help sharpen and strengthen your character.

Consider the story of my friends, Mark and Andrea. Mark works for a successful automotive company and leads a small group ministry at their church. He has a positive, can-do attitude that I admire. Whenever I've faced challenges and shared them with Mark, he always listens and encourages me by saying that we can handle it.

Two weeks after they had their first baby, Mark left a note for Andrea with some reminders for the day and a seemingly odd message at the bottom: "think about your hobby." Andrea was puzzled and even frustrated by the comment. Throughout the day, she kept looking at the note, wondering what Mark meant by it and whether he thought she had too much free time on her hands.

Later that afternoon, when Mark called Andrea, she

asked him about the note. Mark laughed and explained that he had actually written, "think about your hubby." This simple misunderstanding shows how our thoughts and attitudes can sometimes lead us astray and create unnecessary stress in our lives.

A wrong attitude can hijack and captivate your thoughts and life, much like the misunderstanding in the story of Mark and Andrea. A negative attitude is as disabling as worry, which is like fear on a treadmill—a constant cycle of unproductive thinking.

No one will give you a positive attitude; you have to develop it yourself. A positive attitude helps catch happiness and provides the resilience needed in life. For instance, when faced with a rude person, maintaining a positive attitude ensures that one person's behavior doesn't ruin your day. It's essential to recognize that when you say, "You make me mad!", you're allowing others to control your attitude and, in turn, your life. Reacting to others puts you in a position of weakness rather than impact.

A positive attitude is crucial for success in various aspects of life, whether it's in a company, a church, or a home. We have a choice every day regarding the attitude we embrace, and we can't change our past or how others behave. Life is 10% what happens to us and 90% how we react to it. It's up to us to take charge of our attitudes.

Take a moment to reflect on this important question: "What will be the attitude of my life?" Consider how you can cultivate a positive attitude and make a lasting impact on your life and the lives of those around you.

Life also requires intentionality.

Intentionality is crucial for building a spectacular life. Understanding your purpose and what you intend to do each day will help you approach each morning with excitement and motivation.

Sometimes, we get caught up in the language of goals, visions, missions, and strategies and forget to ask ourselves what we intend to do. Reflect on what you want to achieve today, tomorrow, this week, or this month.

A powerful phrase to help connect intentions with impact is: "I know I'm being successful when..." This phrasing focuses on the present rather than treating success as a destination. If the word "successful" carries a negative connotation for you, substitute it with "effective": "I know I'm being effective when..."

In working on personal goals, it's essential to define your roles in life and consider what you want to achieve in each capacity. Writing down your intentions is vital for clarity. If you're not clear about what you intend to do, be, or have, it's challenging to make progress towards your goals.

Remember, intentionality is the key to making the most of your life and achieving the success you desire.

When your intentions fail or you don't accomplish what you intended to do, consider it an experiment. Life is full of experiments, and it's essential not to let setbacks deter you from making progress. Thomas Edison, after losing his laboratory to a fire, considered the disaster an opportunity to start anew. Use your mistakes as stepping stones rather than stumbling blocks.

Remember that what lies behind you is nothing compared to what lies within you and ahead of you. By focusing on positive attitudes, setting clear intentions, and managing your life effectively, you can create momentum and make a significant impact.

Management is a crucial part of taking AIM in life. The poem presented above reminds us of the importance of self-reflection and understanding the duality of our identities. Are we managing our lives well? We'll know if we are when we face storms and crises, which are inevitable in life.

To successfully navigate life, focus on cultivating a positive attitude, being intentional about your goals, and managing your time and resources effectively. Embrace challenges as opportunities for growth, and remember that you have the power to shape your life and achieve your aspirations.

Life takes management, which involves moving towards your strengths, managing your weaknesses, and staying focused on your goals.

Imagine if you were chosen to participate in the Olympics. This would be a life-changing opportunity, and you would likely become consumed with preparing for the race. You would recognize that this is your chance to achieve greatness, and your passion for success would drive you every day.

The same principle applies to our lives. We all have a race to run, a purpose to fulfill, and unique talents and skills to develop. By embracing this purpose and passionately pursuing it, we can make the most of our lives and achieve our goals.

To finish well, we need to have the right attitude, clear intentions, and effective management of our resources and time. It is essential to stay focused on what truly matters and dedicate ourselves to our passions and goals.

So, think about the race you were created to run. What is your purpose? What do you want to achieve in your life? Embrace this purpose, and passionately pursue it with the right attitude, intentionality, and management. This is your chance of a lifetime. Make the most of it, and strive to finish well.

In summary, making an impact in your life requires commitment, attitude, intentionality, and management. When you face challenges or pursue new opportunities, it is crucial to manage your time, finances, skills, and relationships effectively.

Remember, the moment you commit to a goal, you open the door for opportunities, resources, and support to flow towards you. Commitment can ignite a chain of events that can help you achieve your goals and make a significant impact in your life.

So, embrace the challenges and opportunities that come your way. Make a commitment to maintain a positive attitude, write down your goals and intentions, and manage various aspects of your life effectively. When you take aim at your life with determination and dedication, you are more likely to hit the center of the mark and achieve great success.

Remember, your life is your race to run, and your purpose is your gold medal. Commit to it, train for it, and manage your life around it. This is your chance of a lifetime, and when you truly commit, you will be well on your way to living a spectacular life.v

15

THE END OF THE BEGINNING

I hope you have enjoyed our journey together. Each of these amazing coaches has taken the time to pour a great deal of their spirit into their chapter. We know that this is only the beginning. You can't transform from a single chapter, but you can begin your journey.

If there was a chapter that stood out for you, now is the time to go deeper with that author. Visit their website, read their other books and see if this is the beginning of something truly transformational for you.

This has been an amazing journey for me and I hope you've learned as mush as I have. I'm already changing many areas of my life as I know that success is a journey rather than a destination. We are on this one together.

I can't wait to see how your life moves forward.

FOUND A TYPO?

While every effort goes into ensuring that this book is flawless, it is inevitable that a mistake or two will slip through the cracks.

If you find an error of any kind in this book, please let me know by visiting:

CelebrityGhost.com/typos

I appreciate you taking the time to notify me. This ensures that future readers never have to experience that awful typo. You are making the world a better place.

ONE LAST THING

Reviews are the lifeblood of any book on Amazon and especially for the independent author. If you would click five stars on your Kindle device or visit this special link at your convenience, that will ensure that I can continue to produce more books. A quick rating or review helps me to support my family, and I deeply appreciate it.

Without stars and reviews, you would never have found this book. Please take just thirty seconds of your time to support an independent author by leaving a rating.

Thank you so much!

To leave a review go to ->

https://celebrityghost.com/transformation

Sincerely,
Jonathan Green
CelebrityGhost.com